THE HEMINGWAY MONOLOGUES:

An Epic Drama of Love, Genius and Eternity

THE HEMINGWAY MONOLOGUES:

An Epic Drama
of Love, Genius and Eternity

PART THREE
DEATH IN THE AFTERNOON

A play in two acts

BRIAN GORDON SINCLAIR

**The New
Atlantian Library**

The New Atlantian Library
is an imprint of
ABSOLUTELY AMAZING eBOOKS

Published by Whiz Bang LLC, 926 Truman Avenue, Key West, Florida 33040, USA.

The Hemingway Monologues: An Epic Drama of Love, Genius and Eternity – Part Three: Death in the Afternoon copyright 2005, 2016 by Brian Gordon Sinclair. Electronic compilation / paperback edition copyright 2016 by Whiz Bang LLC. The cover design and photo was adapted and executed by Michael La Riviere. All photos, unless otherwise noted, are from the mutual collection of Susana Hurlich and Brian Gordon Sinclair.

All rights reserved. No part of this book may be reproduced, scanned or transmitted in any form or by any means electronic or mechanical, including photocopying, recording or any information storage and retrieval system without permission, in writing, from the publisher. Please do not participate in or encourage piracy of copyrighted materials in violation of the author's rights. Purchase only authorized eBook editions.

This work is based on factual events. While the author has made every effort to provide accurate information at the time of publication, neither the publisher nor the author assumes any responsibility for errors or for changes that occur after publication. Further, the publisher does not have any control over and does not assume any responsibility for author or third-party websites or their contents. How the eBook displays on a given reader is beyond the publisher's control.

For information, contact:
Publisher@AbsolutelyAmazingEbooks.com

ISBN-13: 978-1945772122 (The New Atlantian Library)
ISBN-10: 1945772123

*DEATH IN THE AFTERNOON is dedicated to
Michael Haskins*

*As a friend, publicist and fellow author, he has calmed the
rough waters and made for a smoother voyage.*

PERFORMANCE RIGHTS

For the first time, with this publication, performances will be allowed by groups or individuals other than the author. No performance, other than by Brian Gordon Sinclair, may be given unless a license has been obtained from the author. No alterations may be made to the title or the text without prior written permission from the author.

The original production of *Part Three: Death in the Afternoon* was multi-media and used a series of twin slide projections and a soundtrack. For performance purposes, the author, upon request, will provide a previous script with slide and sound effects indicated. The play, in its current form, has been rewritten to eliminate those effects. This revised script retains the original monologue while eliminating the need for costly production components and makes the show extremely portable for travel.

Brian Gordon Sinclair as *Ernest Hemingway*

INTRODUCTION

The *Hemingway Monologues: An Epic Drama of Love, Genius and Eternity* reads like an intimate memoir. A fascinating blend of fact and fiction, the monologues reveal a tender, compassionate side of Hemingway that most people have never encountered. They can be enjoyed readily in performance or as a good, absorbing read.

The Hemingway Monologues

Originally intended to be one play detailing the life of Ernest Hemingway, it became apparent that a life that large could not be contained in one vessel. *The Hemingway Monologues* evolved into a multi-play series.

Death in the Afternoon is the third play of the series. Once again, a stage play illuminates both the writing and the life of Ernest Hemingway in equal measures. *Death in the Afternoon* is a must see – must read production for all lovers of Hemingway's books, for anyone intrigued by his life and death. It is also a superb introduction to Hemingway for the uninitiated.

The Hemingway Monologues consist of seven plays. The first six plays present the Hemingway chronology from birth to death. The seventh play is a special edition compilation (See: "About the Author and His Work" for a synopsis of each play):

1. *Part One: Sunrise*
2. *Part Two: The Lost Generation*
3. *Part Three: Death in the Afternoon*
4. *Part Four: The Man-Eaters*
5. *Part Five: The Death Factory*
6. *Part Six: Sunset (In Deadly Ernest)*
7. *Part Seven: Hemingway's HOT Havana*
   (special compilation edition)

Brian Gordon Sinclair gives an intimate insight into the circumstances which shaped the famed author's life and inspired him in his writing.

Death in the Afternoon debuted at the Hemingway Days Festival in Key West, Florida in July of 2005 in support of the Hemingway Collection at the Customs House Museum administered by the Key West Art and Historical Society. The final performance was attended by the Honourable Anthony Knill, Consul General of Canada.

Brian Gordon Sinclair

Act I:
The play opens with a description of the "Running of the Bulls" in Pamplona, Spain, followed by a dramatization of an actual bullfight. Act One concludes with the critical reactions to *The Sun Also Rises* and Hemingway's farewell to Paris.

Act II:
The second act begins with scenes of Key West and a brawl at Sloppy Joe's Bar. Hemingway gets stranded in the Dry Tortugas, saves his son's life, and plans a rebellion. The act finishes with the devastating hurricane of 1935.

- Brian Gordon Sinclair

THE HEMINGWAY MONOLOGUES:

An Epic Drama
of Love, Genius and Eternity

PART THREE: DEATH IN THE AFTERNOON

ACT ONE

SETTING:
A typewriter, paper, pencils, a small Spanish flag, a whiskey flask, letters, a pistol, a bankbook and a stack of bills rest on a small table, stage left. In front of the table is a steamer trunk with "HEMINGWAY" painted in red across the front. Another table, stage right holds a quilt, muleta (scarlet bullfighting cape), estoque (sword), banderillas (small harpoons), letters, a Key West newspaper and a storm chart. Near this table is a wooden coat rack with a Spanish shawl and a bota (leather wine

The Hemingway Monologues

container). Beside each table is a chair. Other items may be present as additional set decoration.

While the audience enters, bullfight music plays concluding with Espana Cani.

AT RISE:
The house lights fade to black as the stage lights fade up. Hemingway enters at the end of the music, Espana Cani. He is wearing a beret and carrying a pink and yellow capote. He examines the cape, holds it in the proper position to perform a pass called a Veronica and calls to an imaginary bull.

HEMINGWAY
Toro! Toro!

(He swirls the cape as if performing a successful pass, drapes it over his right arm, raises his left arm and shouts.)

Ole!

(He admires the cape, places it on the rack and addresses the audience.)

To be a matador, now that is something to die for. And I ask you this, how many of you are willing to die for your art?

My name is Ernest Hemingway and I'm the son-of-a-bitch who tried to explain bull fighting to the rest of the world. For those of you who think you already know everything, I suggest you take out your flask ...

(He picks up a flask from the stage left table and drinks.)

Brian Gordon Sinclair

... have a little sip and rest your eyes. *Salud!* As for the rest of you, pay attention and I'll give you the true gen.

Pamplona, white-walled, sunbaked, high up in the hills of Navarre. In the first two weeks of July each year, they hold the World Series of bull fighting. Hotels double their prices and the streets are filled with men in blue Basque caps and girls, really beautiful girls, gorgeous and dark-eyed, just like you.

All day and all night they dance solid in the streets to the peasant music of Riau-Riau. It pounds and throbs as fireworks and rockets explode over your head in a blinding burst. It is impossible to sleep and just when you think you might it is daylight and there is a crash of music in the street below. It is five o'clock in the morning and the street is full of people all going in one direction toward the great public square. It is *encierro*, the running of the bulls, and it commences at six a.m. That is when they let the bulls out into the streets.

We followed the crowd into the bullring, the new concrete bullring and mounted to the top, close to the yellow and red Spanish flag blowing in the early morning breeze. There were easily twenty thousand people there.

Far away, a rocket exploded. The bulls have been released and are racing through the city. Below, a crowd of men and boys running, running as hard as they could go. Behind them are the bulls. Eight bulls galloping full tilt, black and glistening, their horns bare. With them, three steers with bells on their necks. They all ran in a solid mass, and ahead of them sprinted, tore, ran and bolted the men and boys of Pamplona. They had allowed themselves to be chased through the streets for a morning's pleasure.

One boy in his red sash and canvas shoes with a *bota* hung from his shoulders, tripped as he sprinted down the straightaway. The first bull saw him, lowered his head and made a jerky, sideways toss. The boy crashed up against the fence and lay there limp. The bull rejoined the herd and entered the ring. The crowd roared and the boy lived. That was the entry. And there was a casualty list at least equal to an Irish election.

This time no one was killed but sometimes things do go wrong, like the time in Valencia when a bull stumbled while running through a small village. When he is separated and alone, the bull is afraid and when he is afraid, he attacks. The first thing he saw was an open doorway with a man standing in it. He charged at once, lifted the man clear out of the door and swung him back over his head. Inside, in the bedroom, an old woman sat in a rocking chair. She was deaf and had not heard the commotion. The bull demolished the chair and killed her. The man who had been tossed from the doorway ran back in with a shotgun to protect his wife but she was already lying dead in the corner of the room. He fired point blank but only tore up a shoulder. Then the bull caught the man and this time he killed him. Then he charged his own reflection in a mirror, smashed an armoire and made it out into the street where he met a horse and cart. He killed the horse and overturned the cart. That's when the two steers came up, one on each side, and trotted him quietly away.

Back in Pamplona, a ton of speed and needle sharp horns charged again and again into the packed mass of men and boys in the bullring. It is too jammed for them to climb over the fence and the bull may wound or kill thirty men before they can get him out, like the young man who took eleven *cornadas*. The horn punctured his lung, his liver and his bowels. He lived but not well. That is the chance the Pamplona bullfight fans take every morning during the fiesta. That is the Pamplona tradition. The bulls have one final shot at everyone in town before they face death in the afternoon.

Pamplona is the toughest bullfight town in the world. The amateur fight proves that. About three hundred men with pieces of cloth and old shirts, anything that will imitate a bullfighter's cape, sing and dance in the arena. Out comes a young bull as fast as he can come. On his horns are leather knobs to prevent his goring anyone. He charges, hits a man, tosses him high in the air, and the crowd roars.

Then the bull will turn like a cat and get somebody who has been acting very brave about ten feet behind him.

And every time the bull bags someone the crowd roars with joy. No one is armed. No one hurts or plagues the bull in any way. They are there only to test their manhood and to have fun.

In 1924, Donald Ogden Stewart and I decided to give this amateur fight a try. The result ended up in the newspapers.

(He picks up a paper stage left and reads.)

Here's what the Chicago Tribune said:

"BULL GORES 2 YANKS ACTING AS TOREADORS

It occurred when Mr. Stewart said he could leap on the bull's back and blow smoke in the bull's eyes and then beat him down. The chief toreador presented Mr. Stewart with a scarlet cloak and during the handshaking, the bull rushed for Mr. Stewart, tossed him into the air and tried to horn him. Mr. Hemingway rushed to the rescue and was also gored."

Now here's what really happened...
In Pamplona, we were all excited, drunk, hot or hung over. I had declared myself Ernest de la Mancha Hemingway representing the Stock Yards of Chicago and Donald was my faithful companion. As the tribune said, he was helped into the bullring and handed a red cloak. So there he was standing alone in the middle of an audience of thousands with the bull glaring at him just six feet away. The bull charged and tossed him. But Donald, drunk as he was, struggled right back up and said, "Aw, it was nothing." I clapped him on the back and he told me he felt as if he had scored a winning touchdown.

Now Donald wore glasses and when the bull charged him, the glasses went flying. Half blind, he again challenged a bull he could barely see. "Come on, you stupid son-of-a-bitch, come on." That was a mistake, a very painful mistake.

The second time, the bull caught him with one balled horn and flipped him off onto the other balled horn. He landed right on it and it entered a particular opening in his anatomy. Fortunately, the bull tossed him off immediately. And thank God he was anesthetized with alcohol. He looked up at me with a dumb grin and said, "This must be Christmas, because I just had the biggest goose you can imagine." His pants were ripped right off so I gave him my sweater to cover his ... modesty. He made a skirt out of it and headed back to the hotel with that stiff, broom-up-the-ass kind of walk. I must say he looked rather fetching in his little skirt ... and I didn't let him forget it.

(He returns the letter.)

Don't think it was all a joke though. The same thing happened to a real matador when the bull's horns were not bandaged. When the horn entered his rectum and pierced his guts he was a dead man. That could have been Donald, or me, so from then on I decided to be a hell of a lot more careful. I had no intention of making *The Sun Also Rises* a posthumous work.

At 4:30 it was time for the *entrada*, the entrance of the matadors. Now, I could just describe a bullfight. Instead, I am going to tell you the story of Manuel Garcia but first I need to remind you of the last time we talked. I told you then that on July 2, 1961 I will blow my brains out with that shotgun. In 1924 I had yet not planned this particular exit, but if I had, I would have wanted to go with dignity while I still had the strength to do it. This is the story of a man who did just that, a man who was undefeated.

(He moves the stage right chair to the center and sits.)

It is a story like all stories and all stories if they go on long enough, end in death.

Manuel Garcia was an over-the-hill bullfighter. He had had only one *corrida* that year and it had ruined his leg. Now he was forced to beg and the only thing he could get was a night fight with bulls that no veterinarian would pass in the daytime.

(He stands and moves to the chair by the stage left table.)

The Hemingway Monologues

In those days a good bullfighter would get seven thousand *pesetas*. Manuel was offered three hundred, take it or leave it.

Out of this, he was expected to hire his own *picadors* or else use the cheap ones provided and he knew how bad they were. All he wanted was an even break, to be able to call the shots on the bull and it only takes one good *picador*.

(He sits.)

So again he was forced to beg but not before downing three stiff shots of brandy and falling asleep in a café. When he woke up, his friend, Zurito the *picador* was sitting across the table from him. He told Manuel that he was too old, that he should give it up. But Manuel didn't want to hear that. All he knew was that he had to do it one more time.

(He stands.)

"You watch me," he said, "I've got the stuff." He knew Zurito would *pic* for him. He was the best *picador* living and he was his friend. It was all simple now.

At 10:30 the next night, Manuel had drawn a bull the size of an elephant. He crossed himself and said, "The bigger they are, the more meat for the poor."

(He picks up a brightly colored quilt stage right. It is folded long and narrow. He drapes it over his left shoulder.)

Then they formed up for the *paseo*.

Heads up, swinging with the music, they stepped out, their *quadrillas* behind them. Their gold jackets had seen better times and the pink stockings ... well, I had always been struck by the incongruity of those pink stockings.

Next came the *picadors*, with their steel-tipped lances. Zurito had the only steady horse of the lot.

And finally, the jingling mules with the bull ring servants.

(He opens the quilt for display and drapes it over the end of the stage right table.)

They bowed before the president and dedicated their ceremonial capes to some friend or lovely lady. Manuel had no one so he draped it in front of a stranger and picked up his fighting cape.

(He takes the pink and yellow capote from the rack.)

On the far side of the ring was a red door. It swung open. Inside, it was dark and out of that darkness came a big, black bull weighing over a ton. He came out at ninety miles an hour with plenty of gas. For an instant the sun seemed to dazzle him and he stopped frozen, his horns pointed forward, sharp as porcupine quills. Then he charged. And as he charged, I suddenly saw what bull fighting was all about.

The bull was absolutely unbelievable, like some great prehistoric creature, absolutely vicious and absolutely deadly.

(He performs his first veronica.)

Manuel stepped out on the hard sand and shouted at the bull. *Toro!* He sidestepped and swung his cape in front of the horns.

(He performs his second veronica.)

Without an instant's hesitation the bull charged again. But Manuel stood his ground and floated the cape like a ballet dancer's skirt over the bull's face. *Toro!*

Five times he did this. *Toro!*

(He swirls the cape around himself.)

… until he wound the bull around himself like a belt. *Ole!*

The bull was left facing Zurito. He sunk the point of the *pic* in the hump of swelling muscle and leaned all his weight on it but the bull broke away and charged the other *picador*. He drove his horn into the thigh of the *picador*, and tore him, saddle and all, off the horse's back.

But Zurito had done a good job on the bull. You could see the shine of the blood, pumping red against the black of the bull's shoulder. He was slower now and he was bleeding badly

(He returns the quilt and picks up the banderillas.)

The next act is the planting of the *banderillas*, two and a half foot colored darts with harpoons at the end.

(He approaches an audience member.)

You hold them at arm's length and when the light hits the steel points, it catches the bull's eye. Sometimes, you can trick him by taking a false step, like this.

(He demonstrates and shouts.)

Hah ... hah ... hah!

And then you get the hell out of the way. The *banderillas* flopped like porcupine quills while the bull jumped like a trout.

When the rest of the barbs were placed you could see a rip in the torero's jacket. The horns came that close to his flesh.

(He trades the banderillas for the muleta and sword.)

But all Manuel could think of was his work with the *muleta* and sword.

It was the third and final act.

Manuel dedicated the bull to the President, tossed his hat over his shoulder and walked toward the bull. He knew he could do this. As the bull watched, his legs tightened. *Toro!*

The bull turned like a cat and charged again. *Toro!* Hah! The hot body passed too damn close.

A few more passes and Manuel was ready for the kill. His face was white and sweating. The bull was waiting.

He profiled himself toward the left horn. Lower the *muleta*, keep the head down, go in over the horns, and put the sword all the way into a little spot the size of a five-peseta coin. Make the sign of the cross. *Corto y derecho.* Short and straight. *Corto y derecho* ... Hah!

The Hemingway Monologues

There was a shock. He felt himself go up in the air and the sword flew out of his hand.

(He drops the muleta and sword and falls backward onto the center chair.)

Lying on the ground he kicked at the bull's muzzle until the capes took him away.

The sword was bent. He straightened it on his knee and picked up his muleta.

(He rises.)

Again he approached the bull. He sighted, *Corto y derecho* … Hah! Again there was a shock.

(He drops the sword and muleta and returns to the center chair.)

He hit the sand hard and the bull was on top of him. All he could do was play dead. The bull bumped him, bumped his back, bumped his face and he felt a horn go right between his folded arms. It ripped his sleeve off and then he was pulled clear…
This time he needed a new sword.

(He stands and picks up the sword.)

His face was covered in blood.

(He takes out a bloody handkerchief.)

He wiped it off and the blood covered his handkerchief. Then he shook it in front of the bull. Hah! Hah! The bull would not respond. The damn bull was all bone and he would not move. "The hell with you. I'll show you," he said. He wiped his face with the bloody handkerchief and drove in with the sword. The sword buckled and it shot high up in the air end-over-ending, right into the crowd.

(He demonstrates and kneels in slow motion.)

The first cushion thrown out of the dark missed him. Another one hit him in the face, his bloody face. The next thing that hit him was his sword. They had thrown it back at him.

Bastards! Lousy bastards! Lousy dirty bastards!

He tried to straighten the sword...Ahhh! ... but his wrist was ruined, so he picked up the *muleta,* stepped in and jammed the sharp point into the bull's damp muzzle. Huh!

The bull was on him and as he jumped back he tripped over a cushion.

(He returns to the center chair.)

He felt the horn go in, into his side. He grabbed the horn with his two hands and rode backward holding tight onto the place until he was tossed clear.

He was coughing and feeling broken and gone.

"Give me the sword," he said. "Give it to me."

(He picks up the sword and rises.)

Zurito came over, "Go to the infirmary man. Don't be a

damn fool."

"Get away from me.

(He points the sword at Zurito.)

Get the hell away from me."

The bull was standing there, heavy, firmly planted.

(He moves in.)
"All right you bastard…Hah!"

(He holds his ruined wrist as the sword goes in slowly.)

He felt the sword go in, all the way. Right up to the guard. His fingers and his thumb inside the bull, the blood hot on his knuckles.

(He drops the sword.)

Then he was standing clear looking at the bull going slowly down. He gestured to the crowd. "All right you bastards." And again he coughed. It was a hot and choking cough.

(He sits on the center chair.)

Suddenly he was sitting down looking at…something. It was the dead bull. Feet up. Thick tongue out. Things crawling around on his belly and under his legs. To hell with the bull! To hell with them all! All he wanted was to get up on his feet but he couldn't. He fell down again coughing.

(Rise and walk forward to an imaginary infirmary table.)

(The lights fade to the down stage center area only.)

They pushed him up and carried him across the ring to the infirmary. On the table, they cut away his shirt. Manuel felt tired. His chest was scalding inside. Far off he could hear the crowd and the electric lights hurt his eyes.

Zurito was walking towards him with a pair of scissors. They were going to cut off his *coleta*, his pigtail. They were going to cut off his manhood.

"You can't do a thing like that."

"It's all right," Zurito said, "I was only joking."

"I was going good," Manuel said. "I didn't have any luck. That was all."

They put something over his face. He felt tired, very, very tired.

"I was going good," he said weakly. "I was going great. Wasn't I going good, Zurito?"

"Sure, you were going great."

The doctor's assistant put the cone back over Manuel's face and he inhaled deeply.

(Deep breaths and then they stop.)

There were no more words.

(He picks up the sword and the muleta as the lights return to full.)

The Hemingway Monologues

I am not going to apologize for bullfighting. It is a holdover from the days of the Roman Coliseum. And it is not a sport. It was never supposed to be. It is a tragedy. A very great tragedy. The tragedy is supposed to be the death of the bull ... except when something goes wrong.

(He indicates the sword and muleta.)

And that's how Manuel Garcia ended up as *carne de toro* ... meat for the bulls.

(He returns the sword and muleta.)

Speaking of meat ... if you think this is cruel, I want to ask you a question. What did you have for dinner yesterday? And if it was meat, where the hell do you think that meat came from?

(He turns the center chair backwards and sits.)

When I was a student at Oak Park High School, I was taken to the Stock Yards of Chicago. The stench was overpowering and swarms of flies blackened the air. The odor was so bad that you'd think the whole place was filled with politicians. You know, the kind who take a few dollars under the table to let places like that exist. It was the unmistakable odor of all the dead things of the universe. More cattle than you ever dreamed existed. Large cattle, small cattle, old bellowing bulls and little calves not yet an hour born. Every day, ten thousand head of cattle, every year, ten million live creatures killed and cut up into your dinner.

This constant stream of animals, this great river of death was goaded forward with electric shocks. Over the top of each pen leaned one of the "knockers" armed with a sledgehammer. The instant the animal was knocked down, some of them still kicking and struggling, it was slid out to the killing bed. Chains were shackled around one leg and the body jerked up into the air. Have you ever heard a cow cry? Then the butcher bleeds them. One swift stroke and a stream of bright red comes pouring out. Wading through inch deep, steaming hot blood, the gut man rips out the smoking entrails from the carcass.

No particle is wasted. These once living creatures are turned into glue and fertilizer and gelatin and shoe blacking and they are turned into the steak that you ate at dinner yesterday.

(He rises.)

The fighting bull is raised on a ranch with fifty beautiful cows at his disposal. They graze in the finest pastures, drink the best water, exercise in open fields and they live like kings. When they die, it is quick and it is clean, not the ignominious way your dinner died.

And not like the shameful death that happens to animals in war. Do you remember when I wrote about the quay at Smyrna? Before abandoning the city, the Greeks broke the forelegs of all their baggage animals and dumped them off the quay into the water to drown. Incredible numbers of broken-legged mules and horses, unable to swim, screaming in terror. The same way you would scream if your legs were broken. The kind of screams that echo in your mind forever.

(He moves the center chair stage right.)

Death in war is dirty and shameful. It reveals the worst of human nature. In the bullfight, death is an art. It is a ritual that recognizes a law of nature. And if you do not like to see animals die, at least accept the spectacle for what it is. It is the precise enactment of a more civilized way to face death. Now, if you still do not understand, I will meet you tomorrow, in Chicago, at the slaughterhouse, for lunch.

(He picks up a copy of The Sun Also Rises, stage left.)

Out of all this came my first novel, *The Sun Also Rises*. One of the people who helped me get published was Scott Fitzgerald. He convinced me to cut the first sixteen very self-indulgent pages by telling me not what I wanted to hear but what I needed to hear and he was right. The book was a lot better that way. Unfortunately, Scott kept trying to stick his nose into the rest of the book. I stopped that when I wrote him and told him that I had made a startling plot change.

(He returns The Sun Also Rises and picks up some letters.)

Dear Scott:
The hero, like the Great Gatsby, is a Lake Superior Salmon Fisherman. (It is irrelevant that there are no salmon in Lake Superior.) The heroine is a girl named Sophie Irene Loeb who is giving birth to twins in the death house at Sing Sing. She is also waiting to be electrocuted for the murder of the father of her unborn children. The title, *The Sun Also Rises*, comes from Sophie's statement as she is strapped into the chair and the current mounts ...
By the way, don't try to steal my death house scene. Say, is it true that you have become blind through alcohol poisoning?
   Regards to all yr. family

Brian Gordon Sinclair

Signed ... Herbert J. Messkit

Scott of course, when he was sober, could give as good as he got. Listen to this.

Dear Ernest:
I hear you were seen running through Portugal in used underwear and that you have finished a novel a hundred thousand words long consisting entirely of the word "balls" used in new groupings; and that you are engaged in bootlegging Spanish fly in Biaritz where your agents sprinkle it on the floor of the Casino. Please excuse my bawdiness but I'm oversexed and am having saltpeter put in my Pate de Foie Gras.
   Always affectionately
   Scott

I told him that I was always glad to hear from a brother pederast and that I would quit writing immediately and become a pimp.

(He returns the letters.)

Joking aside, Scott gave me some good advice and when the book was published, it became a favorite of the university crowd. Pamplona and the bullfights were new and exciting and so was the sexual freedom. But not as far as the Legion of Decency was concerned.

(He picks up the book.)

This became the book that everyone was afraid to make into a movie. They said that Lady Brett Ashley was a nymphomaniac and you can't make a movie about a nympho and some guy who'd had a certain appendage shot off.

(He returns the book and picks up some reviews.)

And no, no I cannot name the appendage. There are too many young people in the room. But I assure you, I was trying to become a good Catholic.

It seems that every good review was countered by a bad one. Like this one from Miami:

"If you enjoy the stench of garbage; if you can slake your thirst from a bucket of bilge water and be contented; in short, if your thoughts hover around that region of the human anatomy bounded by the knees and the belt, you will be thrilled by Ernest Hemingway's new novel."

I don't think that fellow liked my book.

And of course there was my mother. You could always count on my mother...for an unkind word. Here's what she said...

"It is a doubtful honor to produce one of the filthiest books of the year. Surely you have other words in your vocabulary besides 'damn' and 'bitch'. Every page fills me with a sick loathing."

She went on to tell me that I needed to find some "real work". I filed that letter with the one she wrote when she kicked me out of the cottage in Michigan.

The fact is, I was getting a lot of complaints. But here is the grand prizewinner.

"Ernest Hemingway is a bottom dwelling, scumbskulled,

low-life, slimy, sickening, gutless, spineless, ignorant, pot-licking, cowardly, pathetic, little weasel."

I can only say one thing. I confess. I confess I have licked a few pots in my time.

(He returns the reviews.)

By now, my divorce from Hadley was official. Pauline and I were finally married, twice, church and civil. I even got complaints about that. Archie MacLeish and his wife Ada were so upset that I had left Hadley for Pauline, they refused to come to the wedding. Here's the reason they gave …

(He picks up some letters.)

"We are completely disgusted with your efforts to persuade the Catholic Church that you were baptized by a priest who walked between aisles of wounded men in an Italian hospital – and therefore, you are a Catholic, Hadley has never been your wife and your child is a bastard. To see this farce solemnized by the Catholic Church is more than we can take."

And as usual my parents had to get their licks in too:

"I wish all the 'love pirates' were in Hell. Our family has never had such an incident before. Make your get-away from that individual who split your home. Oh Ernest, how could you leave Hadley and Bumby? Put on the Armor of God and shun Evil Companions."

I did not tell Pauline what a warm impression she had made on my family.

The Hemingway Monologues

(He returns the letters.)

It was time to leave Paris. I had graduated. Besides, Pauline was pregnant with Patrick and we wanted him to be born in America.

Before I left, I paid a few very special goodbyes, to the Luxembourg Gardens where I had walked and thought, the cafes where I worked and played and created, and to all the museums where I had met Cezanne and Van Gogh...
One morning, I took the train to Auvers sur Oise. That's where Vincent Van Gogh died, a bullet to the chest when he was only thirty-seven. A family named Gachet had offered to show me their collection of his paintings. They were very kind and allowed me to explore on my own. After a good look around, I found myself standing in front of a half open door. That's when I began to feel strange. My heart started to pound. I was shaking and my breath would not come.

Something inside that room was calling me. I pushed open the door and stepped in. In front of me was the portrait of the artist. You know it. You've seen it.

The goddamn hairs on the back of my neck were standing on end. His eyes were staring right into me. Bluer than any blue I had ever known. Then I heard the voice, like a raspy whisper. "I see you and I know you. I know you!"

What the hell did he know? I did not understand. Not then. All I knew was that I had to get outside where I could breathe again.

Suddenly I felt very hungry, so I headed for the *Auberge Ravoux* opposite the town hall and police station. As I stepped toward the restaurant, a young boy of about twelve smashed into me. His eyes were red and wet. He looked more afraid than any child I have ever seen. For a moment, he stood still, then he ran directly into the police station.

(He sits stage right.)

I was curious so I sat on a bench and waited. A few minutes later, two gendarmes came out dragging the boy. They threw him into a car and sped away. It seemed my curiosity would have to wait.

Inside I had a delicious lunch, *Blanquette de Veau et Champignons Limon*. That's stew to you. The only thing that spoiled it was when they told me that Vincent Van Gogh had died in the upstairs room.

(He rises.)

After lunch, I left and headed for the train station. On the way, I met one of the policemen.

"Excusez-moi, Monsieur le Gendarme," I said and explained that I had seen him with the young boy.

"Can you believe it?" he said. "A boy runs away from a reform school and the first place he comes to is the police station?"

"What did he want?"

"He claimed that the Christian Brothers had done terrible things to him."

"What kind of things?"

"You are a grown man Monsieur but I cannot repeat them. They were sexual things. They were such filthy things that I had to hit him to shut him up."

"What happened when you took him back?"

"Brother Andre held him in his arms and said, 'We're going to look after you better than you've ever been looked after before."

"Did the boy say anything?"

"No Monsieur, it was disgusting. He just stood there and pissed himself, all over the polished floor. That's when he was dragged away, squealing like a little girl. Good riddance, say I."

I thanked the gendarme for his version of the story and told him I hoped we might all learn something from it.

Instead of catching the train, I found a taxi and went directly to the school where I asked for Brother Andre. I told him what I knew but he denied it, so I took him into a private chapel and I slapped him. I didn't punch him, I slapped him, several times. I told him that I was a reporter and if he didn't bring the boy right away, this story would be in every newspaper in the world. He brought the boy. The kid was trembling but I managed to get him back to the restaurant where the owners looked after him until a good family took him in. They were kind people and they did their best but the boy never got over his wounds, wounds that came from a different kind of war than mine.

Years later, in 1944, he stepped out in front of a German

patrol hurling nothing but stones and insults. They pointed their guns at him and he just stood there and died. It was 4:30 in the afternoon. He never even tried to run. I think he was afraid to kill himself so he got someone else to do it for him. Sometimes, it is very hard to be a Catholic.

(He picks up the flask.)

It had been a hell of a day and it was definitely time to leave Paris. See you in Key West, Florida.

(He toasts, drinks and exits. Lights fade to black.)

END of ACT ONE: INTERMISSION
Music: *La Mer*

THE HEMINGWAY MONOLOGUES:

An Epic Drama
of Love, Genius and Eternity

PART THREE: DEATH IN THE AFTERNOON

ACT TWO

(As Hemingway enters, an instrumental version of the Isle of Capri, is playing. When the lights adjust, the music fades and he addresses the audience.)

HEMINGWAY
Sloppy Joe's was jammed to the sidewalk. Men in dungarees and old service hats crowded the bar three deep. The loud-speaking nickel-in-the-slot phonograph was playing "Isle of Capri".

Boom! A man came hurtling out of the open door, another man on top of him. They fell and rolled on the sidewalk and the man on top, holding the other's hair in both hands, banged his head up and down on the cement. It made a sickening noise.

The sheriff ran over and grabbed him.
"Cut it out," he said. "Get up there."
The man straightened up and looked at the sheriff.
"For Christ sake, can't you mind your own business?"
The other man, blood in his hair, blood oozing from one ear, and more of it trickling down his face, squared off at the sheriff.
"Hey, leave my buddy alone. What's the matter? Don't you think I can take it? Say, could you lend me a buck?"

(Move behind the stage right table.)

Up at the bar a vet was arguing with Josie Russell about the payment of a drink.
"You're a goddamn liar," he said.
"Eighty-five cents," Josie said and spread his hands on the bar.
"You're a goddamn liar," said the Vet and picked up a beer glass to throw. As his hand closed on it, Josie's right hand swung in a half circle over the bar and cracked a big salt cellar alongside the Vet's Head. He fell forward on his knees and then rolled slowly over, his head in a pool of blood.
"This round's on the house," Josie said. "Put that fellow over against the wall."

(Move center stage.)

On a big night, I've seen a dozen men laying against that wall over there. There was so much blood, you had to mop it up with a bucket.

(Move stage left.)

Over at the bank a man came running out with a gun in his hand. Two more men came out carrying leather brief cases and guns and ran in the same direction. The fourth man, a big one, came out holding a Thompson gun, and as he backed out of the door the bank siren rose in a long breath-holding shriek and the gun muzzle jumped and jumped and fired and fired.

The man turned and ran, stopping only to fire at a bank guard coming out the door. The bullets whacked his chest like three slaps. He slid down on his knees, his eyes wide, his mouth open, as if he was trying to say…

(He imitates the victim.)

"It was a typical, ordinary day in Key West."

(Move center.)

I loved that place from the moment I arrived. There was an outlaw lifestyle that made you feel free. I could drink absinthe all night, tell a few lies, and the next day nobody

gave a damn. Most of the time, I wore an old fishing sweater with khaki pants and a rope belt...
Hell, the most formal I ever got was putting on underwear. And, as usual, the local gossips complained. One old lady said I always looked like I'd just pulled my pants on and planned to take them off again any second. You know the type. There's always a man hiding under her bed.

(He moves towards the typewriter.)

At first no one believed me when I said I was a writer and later, when they did believe me, it didn't matter because nobody had read my books anyway. Down at the turtle kraal, I overheard one of the local Conchs talking about me. He said, "I don't see nothing smarter about that guy H'a'mingway than anybody else but they say he's one smart son-of-a-bitch. He sure don't look it though, but he can sit down to a typewriter and come up with a thousand bucks. Hell, that's more'n I make in a whole year." Everybody else thought I was either a bootlegger or a dope peddler from up north.

(He picks up The Sun Also Rises and In Our Time from the stage right table.)

And the scar on my forehead, from a falling skylight by the way, only added to the image. Finally, I got my publisher, Max Perkins to send copies of my last two books. At least they could read ...Well, they could look at the covers.

(Return the books.)

Brian Gordon Sinclair

Key West had everything I needed ... a beer joint, one good restaurant, a beer joint, a filling station, a beer joint, oh, and a big frame house with girls in the doorway and sailors waiting in the street. Don't know what that was for. Then there was a beer joint and two barbershops on the main street but I didn't use either one. I had my own tonsorial parlor. My wife, Pauline, cut my hair. After all, it was the depression. Did I mention there was a beer joint? Five in all, but my favorite was run by a fellow named Josie Russell.

His hole in the wall served up whatever liquor a man could name, illegal liquor right off the boat from Havana.

I enjoyed the feeling of being far away from everyone who knew me or cared what I did, where Pauline and I could live well on five dollars a day and where I could fish more than I had ever fished in my life. So imagine my surprise when I heard my father's voice calling me. I was fishing near the ferry docks when my parents arrived on the 4:30 ferry from Havana. Neither of us knew the other was in Florida and they had to leave that evening. Mother spent the entire time talking about her new painting career but before they left we did manage to pose for a photo by my new brand new Ford.

I noticed how frail and grey my father looked and then he was gone.

Right afterwards, I met Charles Thompson whose family owned half the businesses on the island. He liked to fish as well as any man in Key West and offered to take me out in his boat. All it took was that first tail-dancing tarpon, rising up out of the water like some silver dream, gill plates rattling and jaws shaking the hook, but I was the one who was hooked. This was not trout fishing. This was enough to make a man forger about trout fishing.

(Pick up a letter stage left.)

What I could not forget though were my family responsibilities. A letter arrived from France informing me that my son from my first marriage needed a change. His mother said:

"Bumby is suffering from coughs and the grippe. He needs some Key West sunshine, not the filthy weather of a Paris winter."

He sailed on the *Ile de France* with his mother and I picked him up in New York. I hadn't seen Bumby for nine months and was looking forward to getting reacquainted on the train trip south.

(He returns the letter and picks up a telegram.)

It was not to be. As the train left Trenton, New Jersey, the Pullman porter brought me a ten-word telegram from my sister Carol who was visiting in Key West. It had been relayed up the line from Penn Station:

"FATHER DIED THIS MORNING ARRANGE TO STOP

HERE IF POSSIBLE."

My throat knotted up and I couldn't speak. After what seemed like a long time, I made a decision.

(Return the telegram.)

I decided to go directly to the funeral in Oak Park. I felt guilty as hell so I knelt down and explained to Bumby that I had to go to see *Grandpere* who was very sick and that he must go on to Key West and he must also obey the porter who would look after him.

"Yes, Papa," he said, "I will do just as you say, I will do just as the black Monsieur says. You will find me a very big man as Mama has told me to be."

It was Bumby's first time in America and I was really worried about leaving him alone on a Pullman, but I didn't believe I had a choice. I was not going to subject him to a funeral with a bunch of relatives he hardly knew.

(Move the stage left chair to the right side of the table and sit.)

My father was a doctor. He knew he was suffering from angina pectoris. Some days the pain was unbearable but he thought he could treat himself. All he succeeded in doing was replacing a good diet with vials of medicine. When the attacks became more frequent, his feet started to hurt. He had diabetes and he was neglecting it. Gangrene was

The Hemingway Monologues

already setting in but he told no one and he wouldn't even get himself checked.

On December 6, he came home at noon looking weak and exhausted. He asked about my kid brother Leicester. Les had a cold but he was sleeping.

"Then I'll just lie down until lunch," he said. "Call me when it's ready."

(He stands.)

Slowly and hanging onto the banister railing, he made his way upstairs.

(He picks up the pistol.)
He closed the bedroom door and took out my grandfather's Smith and Wesson revolver. He placed the barrel behind his right ear and shot himself. The bullet pierced his brain and he died instantly.

(He returns the pistol.)

What nobody knew at the time was that my father was broke. He had lost his savings on some bad real estate in Florida and had mortgaged the house to keep up the payments. If he was too sick to work, everything would be lost. He needed the insurance money for his family

When I arrived home, my mother had been sedated, so I took charge of the situation. I led the family in the Lord's

Prayer in the music room where father was lying and arranged for the service at the First Congregational Church. In the obituary I simply said that he had befriended hundreds in distress.

Before the funeral, I gave my little brother a pep talk. "I don't want any crying, understand, kid? There'll be some who will but not in our family. We're here to honor him for all the people he helped, so I want you to pray as hard as you can, to help get his soul out of purgatory. There's plenty of heathens around here who think you just die and that's it. What they don't seem to understand is that things go right on from here, so you pray for Papa, all right? Les nodded and said he'd try his best.

(Sit at the stage left desk which has a bankbook and stacks of bills. The stage lights narrow to this area.)

That night, I sat alone in my father's office and sorted through his papers. This man who kept records of everything had not balanced his bankbook in months. There were stacks of unpaid bills and overdue taxes. If he had asked me, I would have given him the money. I would have given him anything.

In my mind, I began a long and lonely journey. My father became what he was when I was very young. I held his hand and we walked through the Michigan woods where he named every tree and every flower and he showed me how to catch trout and cook them over an open fire...and my heart was destroyed by tenderness for him. That's when I remembered the question a young boy had asked his father, a long time ago.

"Is dying hard, daddy? No son," he said, "I think it's pretty easy. It all depends."

Right now, it didn't look very easy to me.

On his desk, tucked away in a corner, was a copy of a poem that he'd sent me, this from a father who had never found much good in my writing. It wasn't a great poem but it made up for everything.

"My son,
I can't seem to think of a way
To say what I'd like most to say
To my very dear son
Whose book is just done,
Except give him my love and "HOORAY."

Thank you, Papa.

(He returns the poem and stands.)

They say that men shouldn't cry. I say, "Never be ashamed of an honest emotion. It's okay for a man to cry. Just don't do it in public."

(Full lights.)

When I returned to Key West, I needed some serious

comforting from Pauline and I really needed some serious fishing to help me forget.

That's where Bra Saunders came in. Bra was a true conch and he took me out trolling every day in his big, slow-chuffing Palmer engine boat. It wasn't long before I wanted more. I wanted to try the Dry Tortugas, sixty-five miles westward.

Bra and I rounded up a writer friend, John Herrmann, who had a great sense of humor. We stocked up on booze and lots of ice and, to prevent scurvy, we threw in a few limes and set out. Pretty soon we were more oiled than the engine. With a bottle of Bacardi in one hand and a glass in the other, we all began singing. Say, does anyone here know the operatic version of, "We're in the outhouse now?" And don't ask me to sing it for you. Whenever I sing, nobody realizes I'm singing. They always think somebody in the next room is strangling a cat.

Anyway, the fishing was excellent and we were having a great time. Of course, that's when bad things start to happen, like the day at Fort Jefferson when Bra's boat refused to run. Something had cracked and repair parts were available only in Key West.

Now I want you to understand something. The Dry Tortugas are called dry because there's no fresh water. Many have perished there from thirst. Bear this in mind because I'm the one who told them to leave me behind.

All Bra had was a Johnson outboard and three people would be too much for it. I told them to make a quick trip and get back by tomorrow evening. Without water, I was depending on them.

Oh, they made it to Key West all right and then the fun began. To celebrate, they had a few quick ones and we all know that a quick one is just about the slowest thing on earth. When tomorrow arrived, there was no sign of them. By the next night I was getting damn hungry and starting to feel sorry for myself. All I could do was to do was to lie on the beach and let my eyes roam over the heavens.

(Sit stage right. The lights narrow.)

Now there was a book I didn't write. The book of the sky. Every night a different page and every page, a different story to tell.

Over there is the Southern Cross, the traveler's friend and up there, right across the sky is the Milky Way, the mighty Milky Way.

Do you know what it's made up of? My Irish friend, Chink Dorman-Smith told me. "Souls," he said, "the souls of the dead." That's what the Irish believe and they just might be right. When we die, our souls fly up there to join those who've gone before us. We get in line to enter heaven and every star you see is a soul waiting its turn to go through the gates of paradise. Can you imagine how many millions of souls went to make up that vast highway in the sky? We're all heading for a place on that road of souls. The only question is, "When do we go?"

My father had gone on ahead and was up there waiting for me, but all I knew is that I wasn't ready, not then. Not on that dry August day when I was left alone with nothing but a head full of sky and stars.

(He stands. Full lights.)

Finally, after three days, I heard the boat. When I climbed aboard, I shouted every unprintable, unrepeatable, unmentionable obscenity you can imagine. After their few quick ones, they got the replacement parts and had a few more. After that, it only seemed logical to make a day of it. And, of course, hangovers required eye openers so a new day of celebration followed the first. I could have been dead for all those sons-of-bitches cared. In fact, it was enough to make a man want his own boat.

And what a boat it was. Thirty-eight feet of pure heaven on the water. A cedar and oak beauty with two gasoline engines that could handle any kind of weather. Fast enough to chase a school of fish or save a life if needed. When you opened her up, she damn near planed over the water. By any standards, she was one fine fishing machine.

Pauline said I paid more attention to that boat than I did to her or the kids. Pilar was her name, after a Spanish shrine. It was also the secret nickname I had for Pauline when I was divorcing Hadley.

As for the kids, well not all my trips had the fun and abandonment of the Dry Tortugas. Sometimes they were downright dangerous. They were supposed to be fun but when one of your sons almost dies, you tend to get a little upset.

Some years later, all three of my boys came fishing with me ... Jack ... who did not want to be called Bumby any more. Patrick, whose very difficult birth gave me the ending for *A Farewell to Arms*, and Gregory. This story is about Gregory, my youngest boy or Gig as we called him.

Gig was built like a pocket battleship, a reduced version of me. Behind that smiling face was a dark side that nobody else understood. We recognized it in each other and knew it was bad and I respected it. Gig was born to be wicked but was being very good. The others knew it and he knew it. He was just being good while the badness grew inside him. But I loved him. He was my son and I loved him.

I will never forget the time I had to prove that love. On this particular trip, the morning fishing had been lousy, so we decided to go spear fishing right on the edge of the Gulf Stream. None of that modern stuff with air tanks, just goggles and good, old fashioned, homemade spears. Mostly, we speared yellow tails and snappers and grunts. Grunts are those funny, little ones. When you take them out of the water, they make an almost human sound, bit like a belch.

Most of the fish were harmless and swam in big schools,

thousands of them, but sometimes a barracuda would get closer than you wanted. The main danger from cudas comes when you enter the water too suddenly. They'll slash at you and run off but not before nodding at you, with a piece of your thigh in their mouth.

By this time, Gregorio Fuentes was my first mate. He'd take the dinghy part way out from the Pilar and pull the fish off the boys; spears. The two older boys were tall enough to touch the reef bottom but Gig was only four and a half feet tall. He had to expend a lot of energy just staying afloat. That's when he came up with what he thought was a very clever idea for storing the fish. He unbuckled his belt, put one end in the mouth of the fish, pulled it out through the gills, and then re-buckled it. This way, he could catch three or four fish before having to make the fifty-yard swim back to the dinghy.

After spearing four grunts, he suddenly noticed there wasn't another fish in sight. How could that many fish disappear that fast? Then he saw why. Three huge sharks, each more than eighteen feet long were coming toward him in slow S-shaped curves. The scent of fish blood was calling them.

Gig screamed, uncontrollably, again and again, more terrified than he'd ever been in his life. Even over the sound of the waves, I heard him.

"What is it, Gig?"

"Sharks, sharks," he cried, "three big ones!"

"Okay, pal, take it easy," I said. "Throw something at them to get their attention and swim to me."

He pulled the grunts off his belt and tossed them toward the sharks. Now, Gig wasn't much of a swimmer but this time, he set a new record in getting to me. I hoisted him up on my shoulders, which were barely out of the water with his weight, and started thrashing towards the dinghy. It was my body that was exposed under the surface. They would get me first, not Gig. Sure I was scared but I had to save him. Gig snuck a look back and saw the sharks devour the grunts. Then they turned and started towards us again. Finally, I made it to the edge of the dinghy. Gregorio pulled Gig in and then they both hauled me aboard, just at the exact second when that first shark slapped up against the side of the boat. Phew!

Later, when Gig told me about the dead fish on his belt, I gave him one hell of a bawling out but it didn't matter. My boy was alive and he knew that I cared.

I don't think I could bear to lose one of my children.

(He picks up letter stage right and moves to center stage.)

In 1935 Gerald and Sarah Murphy weren't so lucky. When I was getting divorced from Hadley, they let me live in Gerald's studio in Paris. They were good to me and I was devastated when their eldest boy died. Baoth was only fifteen but he'd had tuberculosis for a long time. Then he caught a bad case of the measles which turned into a brain inflammation. What followed were days and nights of dull horror, one operation after the other, one transfusion after the other. Baoth Murphy died from meningitis with Gerald crying beside him and Sara, leaning over him, pleading, "Breathe, Baoth, please breathe." All I could do was write to them:

(The lights narrow to a center spot.)

"Dear Sara and Dear Gerald,

If Bumby died, we know how you would feel and there would be nothing you could say. Yesterday I tried to write but I couldn't.

It is not as bad for Baoth because he had a fine time, always, and he has only done something now that we all must do. He has just gotten it over with.

It is your loss, more than it is his, so it is something that you can legitimately be brave about. But I can't be brave about it and in all my heart, I am sick for you both.

We all have to look forward to death by defeat, our bodies gone, our world destroyed, but it is the same dying we must do, while he has gotten it all over with, his world all intact and the death only by accident.

Very few people ever really are alive and those that are never die, no matter if they are gone. No one you love is ever dead.

We must live it, now, a day at a time and we must be very careful not to hurt each other.

ERNEST"

(He returns the letter. Full lights.)

Back in Key West, things were pretty bad too. The depression had hit hard. Three out of every four people were on relief. Garbage, uncollected by unpaid workers, was piling up everywhere and with the Army and Navy bases closed, even bars and prostitutes were short of customers. Most of the have-nots were living off nothing but fish and handouts and the number one song on the radio was, "Brother, can you spare a dime?"

(He picks up a newspaper stage right.)

But the real news was that the city and the state had gone broke. It was the banner headline in the Key West Citizen:

"KEY WEST NOW UNDER STATE CONTROL
PASSES INTO HANDS OF FERA
IN REHABILITATION PROGRAM
STATE ADMINISTRATOR JULIUS F. STONE ACCEPTS
GOVERNOROR SHOLT'S INVITATION TO TAKE
CHARGE OF AFFAIRS IN EMERGENCY OPERATIONS"

Well, hallelujah, FERA had arrived, President Roosevelt's

Federal Emergency Relief Act. Now, I was going to be rehabilitated by some son-of-a-bitch who thought he was God. Julius Stone was going to save Key West and he didn't give a damn who he offended. Here's what he said:

"With a scratch of my pen, I started this work and with a scratch of my pen, I can stop it, just like that."

(Return the newspaper.)

Stone was turning Key West into a tourist trap. My quiet fishing town was suddenly filled with horse races, beauty contests, and fireworks. You couldn't even fish off the docks any more. Every day a goddamn brass band marched down and met the ferry from Havana.

Things were so bad that over at Whitehead Street, I had to build a wall around the beautiful new house we had fixed up. It was supposed to be a quiet place to work but half the visitors to the island thought they could walk in and get an autograph whenever they felt like it.

At first I wondered how the hell they knew where I lived and then I saw the map. Julius Stone had prepared a map of the city and presented it to each and every tourist. I ranked number eighteen in a list of forty-eight attractions, right behind Johnson's Tropical Grove but just ahead of the lighthouse and aviary.

And things only got worse. I couldn't go outside without being run over by some little old lady on a bicycle. But the final insult was when the tourist apartments started offering rooms with a view of Ernest Hemingway. So much for standing naked on your own balcony.

It was Shine Forbes who came up with a solution. Shine was a local boxer who used to spar with me. One day, when the bell seemed to ring every two minutes, Shine marched out to the tourists at the gate and said, "I's Ernest Hemingway. What you folks want?" When their shock wore off, one of them said, "But you're a negro." "That's right." Shine said, "I's negro, I's Ernest Hemingway and I's here to tell you about this FIBU Wall. "What's an FIBU wall?" someone asked. Shine drew himself up to his full height, which wasn't very full and put a mean look on his face, which wasn't very mean. "I'll tell you what an FIBU wall is."

Then he picked up an old rusty shotgun hidden behind the wall and pointed it right at them. " 'F I be you, I'd move my sorry ass away from this wall before I get the seat of my pants peppered with buckshot."

(He takes a drink from the stage right table.)

Word soon got around that the Hemingway house was not a safe place to visit.

Shortly afterwards, I took even more drastic measures. There was only one way to stop all this gentrification. Key West must secede from the Union. I drew up a battle plan and sent it to John Dos Passos. I knew he would fight tooth and nail for it:

(He picks up letter stage right and reads.)

"A Call To Action

The *coup d'etat* is planned for the day after the navy and marines go. On the first night we massacre the Catholics and the Jews. The second night, the Protestants who have been lulled into a false sense of security by the events of the first evening. The third night we butcher the free thinkers, atheists, communists and members of the lighthouse service. The fourth day, if things aren't going well, we burn the town. The fifth and sixth days are free and members of the party can amuse themselves as they like. On the seventh day we order Archibald MacLeish to write an epic poem about the movement. Late that evening we shoot Macleish as his poem has turned out lousy. You can see how it will all be. Just one hilarious round with everyone busy and happy. At the end of twelve days we raise wages to beat hell and massacre the Poles. Oh, if there is any group we have not offended, we promise to massacre them too.

Let me hear if you are with us.
Ernest"

(He returns the letter.)

I wasn't the only one who didn't prosper from the tourists. Up on Matecumbe Key, rowdy war veterans were creating problems. Earlier, in Washington, D.C., they had gathered from far and wide to ask for their rights as veterans.

Instead, the army ran them out and they ended up down here working on the overseas highway. They were men without women and without much hope and they were treated like garbage, not like men who had fought for their country.

In February they went on strike. All they wanted was decent sanitation and the same wages as civilian workers. The government's answer was to send in the National Guard and beat them into submission.

A week after the strike, one of the vets stepped up on a Duval Street porch and tried to tell people how bad it was on Matecumbe, how they were living in filth. No one listened so he took all his clothes off and tried again, stark naked. What he got for his trouble was a beating and free accommodations at the city jail.

By late August, another storm was brewing, a tropical storm and it was headed in our direction.

(He picks up a storm chart stage right.)

I studied the storm charts but it was too unpredictable. By Labor Day, the storm was east of Bermuda and headed for the keys but not yet at hurricane force. Forty-eight hours later, in the middle of the night, the veteran's camps on upper and lower Matecumbe disappeared when a twenty-foot wave swept right over the island.

(He returns the chart.)

Brian Gordon Sinclair

Earlier on Monday, at 4:30 in the afternoon, someone remembered that hundreds of vets were stranded on the keys and finally sent a train to get them. Three hours later it stopped at Islamorada to pick up stragglers. That's when the storm hit in full force. The entire train just blew away. Six coaches, two baggage cars and three boxcars. Every car in the train turned on its side and filled with water, the passengers still inside.

Over on Windly's Key, women, children, and forty men, half of them vets, formed a human chain in waist-deep water and tried to make it to the rail crossing. They had seen the train go by. Surely it would return. Around them, buildings disintegrated and disappeared. Only three made it to the crossing. They climbed a tree and prayed.

Back in Key West, the barometer on my desk had fallen to 29.55. At midnight, I tried driving down to the Pilar but the car was drowned out so I bulled my way through the wind and rain on foot. I was not going to lose that boat.
(He stands behind the stage right chair.)

On lower Matecumbe Key, hundreds of ragged vets hung onto anything that seemed solid and I do mean anything. A train is coming, they were told. As the wind howled, tents blew away and wooden buildings imploded in the dark.

(He smashes the chair onto the floor.)

There was no place to hide. Next morning Matecumbe was

The Hemingway Monologues

flat. Nothing was left standing. Only the train engine remained on the track. Thirty miles of track were washed out, steel rails warped and twisted.

On Windly's Key, three survivors climbed down from their tree, exhausted and alone. On the bank of Snake Creek, a body turned green in the early morning light. Other bodies are starting to bloat in the mangrove thickets.

(He picks up the stage left chair and sits center stage. The lights fade very slowly to a center spot.)

All the next day, the winds were too high to get out of Key West and there was no communication. By Wednesday morning we had assembled food and water and medical supplies and set out for lower Matecumbe Key. No one was prepared for what we saw there.

You can't begin to imagine it, two women, naked, tossed up into trees by the water, swollen and stinking, their breasts as big as balloons, flies between their legs. Then, by figuring, you locate where it is and you recognize them as the two very nice girls who ran a sandwich place and filling station three miles from the ferry.

Of the three camps, nothing remained alive but seventy veterans who clung in the howling dark to a tank car filled with water. Several hundred other veterans were starting to rot in the blazing sun. The stench was so bad you needed a gas mask. You needed it to face the horror of bodies so ripened in the sun that they burst open when you lifted them. Some of the men had to stop and vomit in the sand. We made five trips with provisions and nothing but dead men to eat the grub.

(The lights return to full as he stands and moves forward.)

The government sent those sad, cheated veterans down there to get rid of them. They got rid of them all right. These dead vets, who were run out of Washington for asking for what was theirs, were dropped stinking into wooden coffins for burial in Arlington Cemetery. The other bodies were cremated, in piles, like cordwood.

Who exactly sent them down to the Florida Keys and left them to die in the hurricane months? President Roosevelt does not come to Florida in the hurricane months. He does not come because there would be great danger, inescapable danger, to him and his property. Veterans are not property. They are only human beings, unsuccessful human beings. All they had to lose was their lives...and they did.

By Saturday, over six hundred bodies were accounted for. Another four hundred remained missing. Two months later, eight civilians and three vets were cremated on the north end of Matecumbe. After that they stopped looking.

(He stands behind the chair as the lights begin a slow fade.)

I didn't know what else I could do, so I wrote about it. And when I did, I remembered the words I had written to the

The Hemingway Monologues

Murphys when their son died:

All we can do is to live it, now, a day at a time and be very careful not to hurt each other.

(The lights fade to black as the tune, "Nothing to Leave but a Song" plays.)

END of PART THREE:
DEATH IN THE AFTERNOON...

... to be continued in Part Four: The Man-Eaters.

Author's Notes

I encourage you to read Ernest Hemingway's treatise on bullfighting, *Death in the Afternoon*, from which the title of this monologue has been borrowed. At the end of Hemingway's book is "An Explanatory Glossary" which will explain all the bullfighting terms. Hemingway's book is an invaluable resource for the presentation of the first act of this monologue.

To understand and appreciate the story of Manuel Garcia, you will have to read Ernest Hemingway's short story, "The Undefeated". To perform the story of Manuel Garcia, you will have to arrange actual bullfighting lessons. If you do not take bullfighting lessons, I suggest that you simply tell the story to the best of your ability without the actual moves. The matador approach will not be possible for certain performers in some situations.

Lighting cues are minimal. Many venues will have no lighting facilities; however, when a traditional theatre is available, lighting will enhance the performance.

As pre-performance research, aside from Hemingway biographies, I suggest you also read:

"Who Killed the Vets"
Ernest Hemingway
The Masses/Key West Reader

The Hemingway Monologues

To Have and Have Not
Ernest Hemingway

The Jungle.
Upton Sinclair

The author in the Hemingway Room
of the Hotel Ambos Mundos in Havana, Cuba.

ABOUT THE AUTHOR AND HIS WORK:

Brian Gordon Sinclair, author of *The Hemingway Monologues*, is a graduate of the National Theatre School of Canada and holds a Master of Arts degree in Theatre from the University of Denver. He also studied at the Royal Academy of Dramatic Arts in London, England,

The Hemingway Monologues

and at the National Film Board of Canada.

Mr. Sinclair's seven play series, *The Hemingway Monologues: An Epic Drama of Love, Genius and Eternity*, has met with considerable critical acclaim, with the first five plays premiering at the Hemingway Days Festival in Key West, Florida. The sixth play, *Sunset* (originally titled, *In Deadly Ernest)*, was commissioned by Museo Hemingway/Finca Vigia and had its world premiere at the Hemingway Colloquium in Havana, Cuba.

The playwright is a dual citizen of Canada and Ireland. His other works include *Easter Rising: The Last Words of Patrick Pearse*, a recreation of the dramatic days in Dublin during the 1916 struggle for Irish freedom. This play is available as an audio book.

A recipient of the Sir Tyrone Guthrie Award for Acting at the Stratford Shakespeare Festival in Ontario, Mr. Sinclair has also received Awards of Distinction from Museo Hemingway and the University of Holguin in Cuba. He has performed in Canada, Cuba, Denmark, England, Norway, Holland, Poland, Spain, the USA and at the Moscow Art Theatre in Russia.

The Hemingway Monologues started in 2003 with *Part One: Sunrise*, where Mr. Sinclair's utterly convincing and evocative portrayal of Ernest Hemingway – as he fished for trout in Michigan, fell in and out of love, survived major shell wounds in Italy toward the end of World War One, then met and fell in love with a Red Cross nurse – had the Key West audiences, during the devastating final death scene, reduced to tears...albeit, preceded by many lighter and humorous moments. The following descriptions are exactly as they appeared in the original opening night programs:

Part Two: The Lost Generation premiered in 2004 and tells of Hemingway's experiences in Petoskey, MI, his early work at the Toronto Daily Star newspaper and his marriage to Hadley Richardson. Hemingway and his wife move to Paris where the fledgling novelist meets Gertrude Stein, Ezra Pound, Pablo Picasso, F. Scott Fitzgerald and others. He is introduced to Spain and the pageantry of the bullfight and finally meets Pauline Pfeiffer, the woman who will steal him away from Hadley. From these experiences, Hemingway writes his first bestseller, *The Sun Also Rises*.

Part Three: Death in the Afternoon (This volume.) previewed before the Consul General of Spain in Toronto in 2005 prior to Key West. Hemingway attends the "Running of the Bulls" in Pamplona, learns of the life and death artistry of the corrida and dramatizes an actual bullfight. The play then moves to Key West and a brawl at Sloppy Joe's bar. Hemingway gets stranded in the Dry Tortugas, saves his son's life and plans a rebellion. The conclusion examines the destruction of the great hurricane of 1935.

Part Four: The Man-Eaters premiered in Key West in 2006 in the presence of the Consul General of Canada. The play explores Hemingway's extra-marital relationship with Jane Mason, reenacts an African safari, explores dictatorship in Cuba and includes a fight with pirates. Hemingway then travels to Spain and the Spanish Civil War. As a war correspondent, he points out the atrocities of war and concludes with a stirring address that commemorates the Abraham Lincoln Brigade.

Part Five: The Death Factory premiered, after several delays, in Key West in 2009. From the joys of absinthe to the appeal of Ava Gardner, Ernest Hemingway turns to the exotic temptations of China and his third wife, Martha Gellhorn. Back in Cuba, he chases U-boats and tracks Nazi spies as a prelude to the European war and flying missions with the Royal Air Force. Whether commanding French freedom fighters or liberating the Ritz Hotel in Paris, Ernest manages to encounter Sylvia Beach, Marlene Dietrich, Pablo Picasso and Mary Welsh (later to become his fourth wife). While serving in "the death factory" that is World War Two, his emotional resources are strained when his first-born son is taken prisoner by the Nazis.

Part Six: Sunset (originally *In Deadly Ernest*) premiered at the 11th International Colloquium Ernest Hemingway in June of 2011 at the Hotel Ambos Mundos in Havana, Cuba. The North American premiere occurred the following year in Key West. The play continues from the end of World War Two and concludes the chronological series. Earnest eagerly awaits the arrival of Mary Welsh and a new marriage. They deal with life in Cuba, Idaho and Italy as Mary runs the household at Finca Vigia, meets movie stars in Sun Valley and copes with her husband's infatuation in Venice. Ernest also shows his love for his middle son, Patrick, before moving on to publish *Across the River and Into the Trees* and *The Old Man and the Sea*. In Africa with Mary, Ernest is involved in two plane crashes that mark a gradual but certain deterioration in his health. After winning the Nobel Prize, he manages to continue writing in spite of the intrusions on his privacy. Eventually, a series of losses, including his beloved Finca Vigia, leads him to the Mayo Clinic and, finally, his demise.

Part Seven: Hemingway's HOT Havana is a special stand-alone edition. It is not part of the preceding six part chronological series. *Hemingway's HOT Havana* is a bold, rousing adventure tale brought to life by author, director and master storyteller, Brian Gordon Sinclair. It includes the following stories as excerpts from the original six plays and rearranged into a unique entertainment: life and crime in Havana ... writing tips for Arnold Samuelson ... Jane Mason ... baseball ... Ava Gardner ... fishing the great blue river ... El Floridita ... the pirates of Havana Harbor ... shark attack ... lions, bears and banderillas...drinking with Hemingway ... German U-boats ... the Nobel Prize ... the death of Black Dog and Machakos ... and a shocking end. The show was originally performed, rough-hewn, in Havana on the rooftop of the former El Pacifico restaurant in 2005 during the precise moment of a total eclipse.

PHOTO GALLERY

The author wears a *capote* obtained in Madrid at *Las Ventas*.

Photo: Charles Bryant

Brian Gordon Sinclair

The author has yet to learn the correct way to hold the *capote*. The major portion of the hand should not be exposed at the front of the cape.

Photo: Charles Bryant

Hemingway On Stage poses with a friend
who dropped by for the photo shoot ...
... no bull!

Photo: Charles Bryant

Brian Gordon Sinclair

Premiere of *Part III: Death in the Afternoon* in Key West with Anthony Knill, Consul General of Canada and Lorian Hemingway, granddaughter of Ernest Hemingway.

Valerie Hemingway (former wife of Gregory Hemingway) and Consul General, Anthony Knill pose after the opening performance.

Brian Gordon Sinclair

A demonstration of the use of *banderillas*
in performance in Key West.

Photo: Alberta Pizzolato

The Hemingway Monologues

With Charlie Boice and Tom Grizzard
in Pamplona, Spain for the Festival of San Fermin and
the Running of the Bulls

50th Anniversary Celebration
Ernest Hemingway: 1959 - 2009

Brian Gordon Sinclair

Hemingway On Stage distributes gifts
to the Gigi All-Stars at
The First Annual Gigi All-Star Exhibition Game
and Holiday Celebration, 2013.

The author tosses a few slow ones at Finca Vigia, 2013.

Brian Gordon Sinclair

Brian Gordon Sinclair tells his favorite story about writers in heaven and hell.

Hemingway On Stage films a speech from *The Hemingway Monologues* and then relaxes for an interview with Honorary Key West Mayor Sammie Mays, 2013.

After an interview with Jenna Stauffer of Good Morning Florida Keys 2013.

With Cayuco, the original Homerun Kid at Finca Vigia.

Brian Gordon Sinclair

The author displays Ernest Hemingway's Nobel Prize Medal in Santiago de Cuba.

OTHER WORKS BY BRIAN GORDON SINCLAIR

The Hemingway Monologues: An Epic Drama of Love, Genius and Eternity
PARTS ONE & TWO

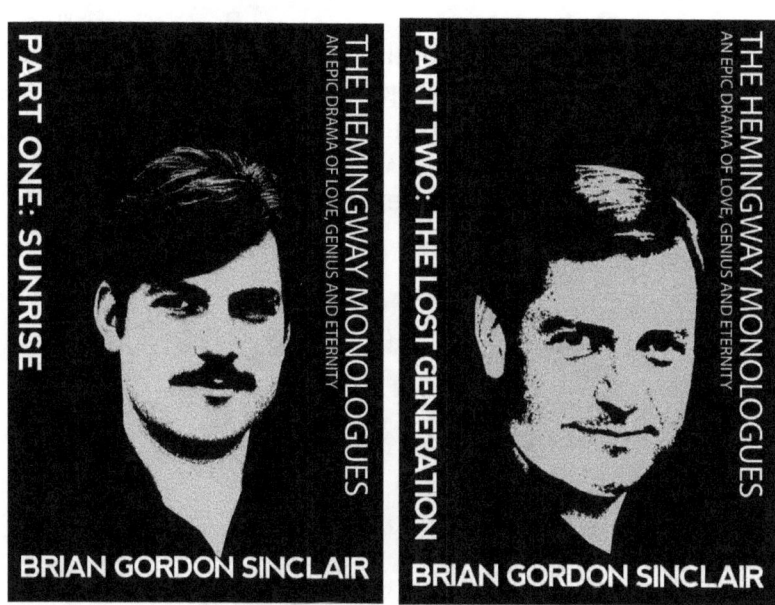

The Hemingway Monologues: An Epic Drama of Love, Genius and Eternity is a seven part dramatic series that reads like an intimate memoir. A fascinating

The Hemingway Monologues

blend of fact and fiction, the monologues reveal a tender, compassionate side of Hemingway that most people have never encountered. They can be enjoyed readily in performance or as a good, absorbing read. *Sunrise* and *The Lost Generation* are the first two plays of a series that traces Hemingway's chronology from birth to death. *The Hemingway Monologues* give an intimate insight into the circumstances which shaped the famed author's life and inspired him in his writing.

The first three volumes of the series, including this one, are now published. The remaining five volumes, to be published in order, will be available soon.

Hemingway's HOT Havana

Soon to be revised, the original cover of *Hemingway's HOT Havana* displayed a composite drawing of Ernest Hemingway and Brian Gordon Sinclair.

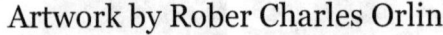

Artwork by Rober Charles Orlin

Brian Gordon Sinclair

Cuba Solidarity in Canada

Cuba Solidarity in Canada – Five Decades of People-to-People Foreign Relations, is a collection of essays about the Canadian solidarity movement in support of Cuba during more than 50 years. Throughout the different experiential stories, the notion of solidarity emerges as the common theme of people-to-people (non-governmental) links between Canada and Cuba. The book suggests a framework that informs the reader on the meaning, positive influence and potentially valuable role that solidarity can play in the relationship between peoples, indeed between nations. It also advances the possibility of a new paradigm of state-to-state foreign relations that is based on solidarity instead of ideological posture. Included is a final chapter by Brian Gordon Sinclair.

Abstract, Chapter 12, *Cuba Solidarity in Canada.*

"Ernest Hemingway: One Canadian's Doorway into Cuba."

I speak not of politics but of love. Ernest Hemingway opened a doorway that allowed me to discover the vibrant love of literature and people that is Cuba. He lived there for twenty years until forced out by America's fear of socialism. His spirit, however, is still there. I know that because when I meet the people of Cuba, as a writer and performer of Hemingway, I can feel it. His spirit exists in the people, in their hearts. Now he has moved into legend. In Havana, in Holguin and in Santiago, I have had the pleasure of sharing that legend. I have portrayed Hemingway at the 50th Anniversary of the meeting of Fidel Castro and Ernest Hemingway. They met at an international fishing tournament organized by Hemingway and where Fidel won the trophy for catching the most fish. I have appeared in Holguin at the Cuban 5 Colloquium while speaking in support of freedom and relishing the joy of a festival called Los Romerias de Mayo and I have appeared in Santiago de Cuba, sharing my work with students at the University of Oriente and participating in the astounding Festival of the Caribbean. In each case, my experience was intensely personal. In each case, Ernest Hemingway led me to and through an island that I did not know, to an island that now summons me to know more, much more.

Brian Gordon Sinclair

Easter Rising: The Last Words of Patrick Pearse

Russia, Spain and Cuba provided three of the four greatest revolutionary dramas of the 20th Century. In 1916 Dublin, Ireland provided the fourth. It was called the Easter Rising and Easter 2016 will commemorate the 100th anniversary of the Rising. *Easter Rising: The Last Words of Patrick Pearse* is a recreation of the original event as told by the commander of the Rebel forces. A new edition, including an audio book version, will be available early in 2016.

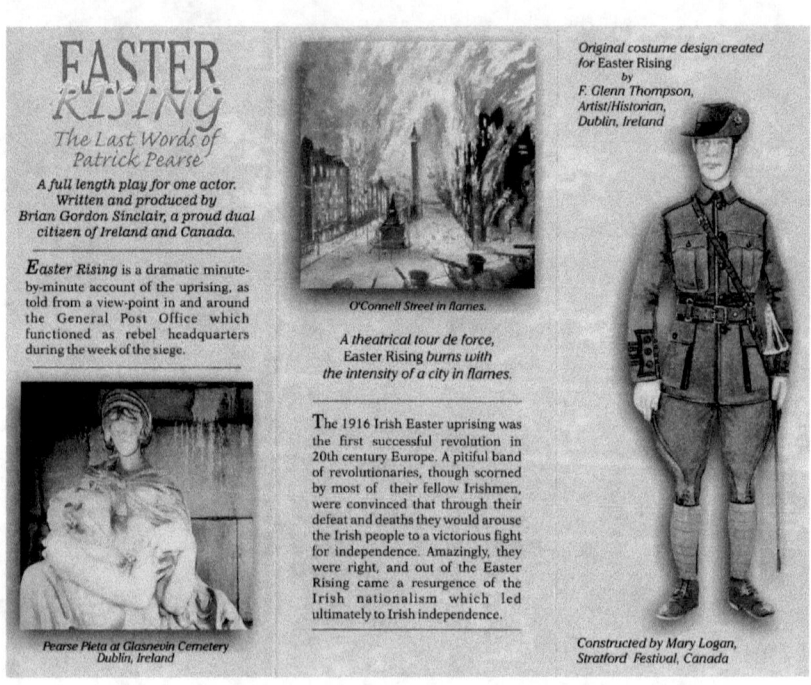

Brian Gordon Sinclair

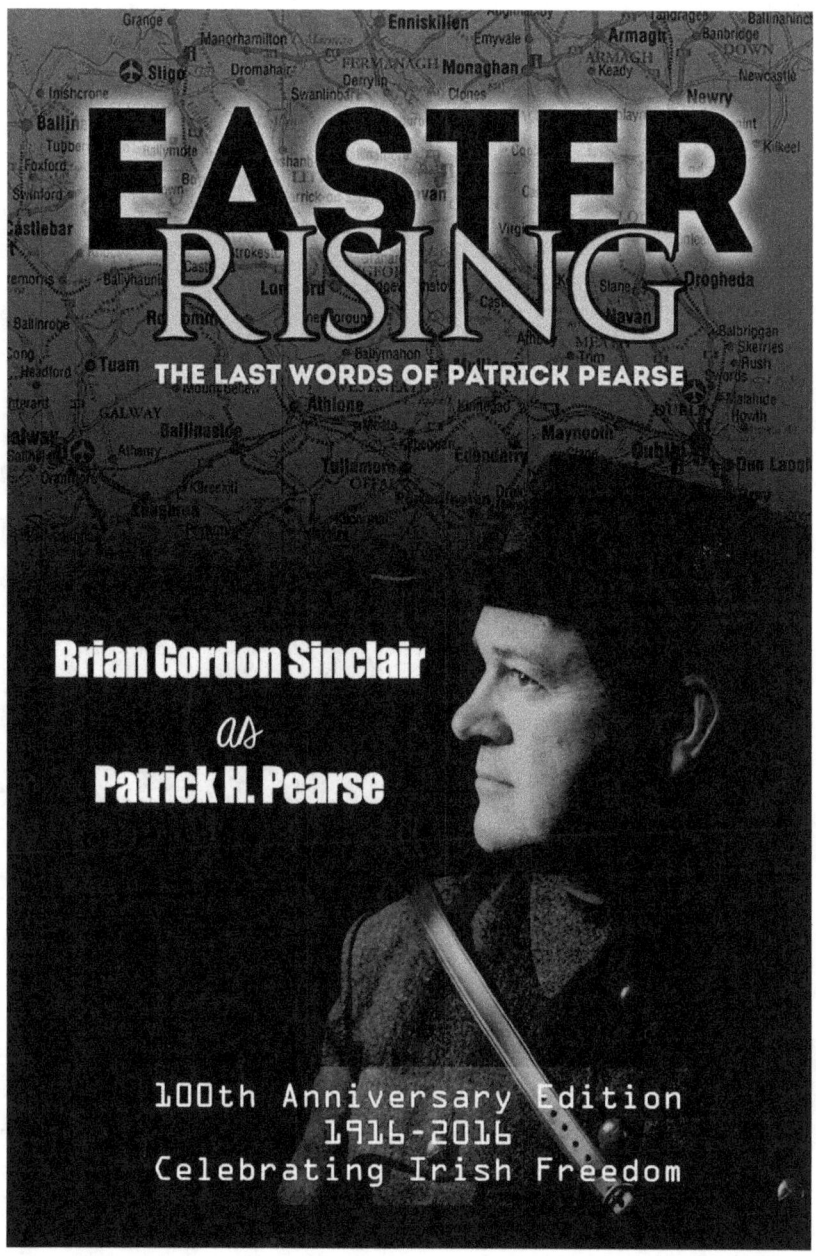

The Homerun Kid: The True Story of Ernest Hemingway's Baseball Team

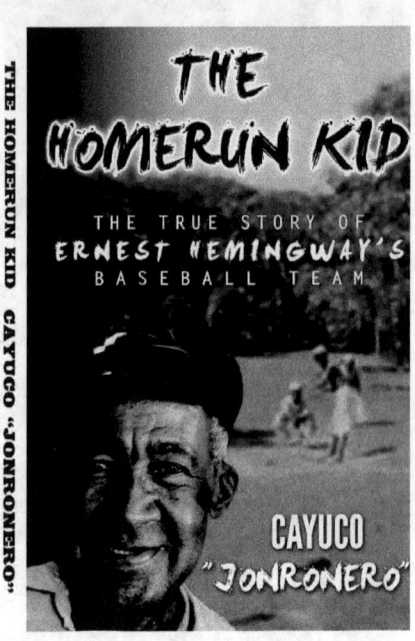

THE HOMERUN KID is a brilliant memoir, told with genuine childhood innocence!

A heart-warming tribute to Ernest Hemingway. You can feel a child's love for his hero permeating every memory, every word.

THE HOMERUN KID is more than a book of children's stories. It is a valuable addition to the history of Ernest Hemingway and offers a vivid, eye-witness account to scholars and aficionados.

THE HOMERUN KID should be read to young people in every library and classroom in the world!

THE ART OF STORYTELLING AT ITS FINEST! From the true stories of Cayuco "Jonronero" the Homerun Kid

Translation by Susana Hurlich
Adapted and edited by Brian Gordon Sinclair
$14.95

Adapted and Edited by Brian Gordon Sinclair
from the original stories of
Oscar Blas Fernandez Mesa.
Translation by Susana Hurlich.

As of this writing, I have completed adapting and editing the memoirs of Oscar Blas Fernandez Mesa, age 86, the only functioning member of the original Hemingway children's baseball team. The book is now available for your reading pleasure.

SPECIAL INVITATION:

ANNUAL EXHIBITION GAME AND HOLIDAY CELEBRATION

Estrella de Guigui / Gigi All-Stars

HISTORY:

In the 1940's, a children's baseball team was formed to provide an activity for Ernest Hemingway's sons when they visited their father. It was named after Ernest's youngest son Gregory, also known as Gig and Gigi. During this time, Hemingway provided uniforms, equipment and drove the kids anyplace they could arrange a game. At Christmas, the children were invited to Finca Vigia (Lookout Farm), the Hemingway estate, where Ernest would tell stories to the children and give each one a present.

Approximately, six years ago, The Director of Museo Hemingway (Ada Rosa Alfonso Rosales) and Oscar "Cayuco" – the Homerun Kid – Blas, the 86-year-old surviving member of the original team, decided to revive the team known as the Estrellas de Guigui/the Gigi All-Stars. It has been my pleasure assist with that revival. In December of 2013 (helped by Papa Wally Collins of the Hemingway Lookalike Society), I not only had the privilege of arranging uniforms and equipment for the team but I also revived the storytelling tradition along with the presentation of a gift to each child. Each player received a card containing one dollar and a copy of the book from which the story was taken. Naturally, the book and story vary from year to year. So far, the children have received copies of *The Hemingway Monologues, The Pirate Night before Christmas* and *The Homerun Kid*. Many more books are to come.

As Patron of the Gigi All-Stars, I invite you to join us for the Annual Exhibition Game and Holiday Celebration. The event is held yearly at Museo Hemingway in San Francisco de Paula on the outskirts of Havana and takes place on the first Saturday of December. Admission to the event is complimentary. Hemingway, baseball, literature, children and Christmas - the perfect combination.

Brian Gordon Sinclair
Patron

QUESTIONS?

Contact Hemingway On Stage

sinclair4814@rogers.com www.briangordonsinclair.com

P.O. Box 337
Alliston, ON, Canada L9R 1V6

The Hemingway Monologues

Annual Exhibition Baseball Game and Holiday Celebration

An Honorary Papa in the Hemingway Look Alike Society, Brian Gordon Sinclair shares a farewell glass of Havana Club with his Cuban friends and members of the society after their participation in the 2nd Annual Exhibition Game and Holiday Celebration, 2014, at the Hemingway Estate, Finca Vigia, in San Francisco de Paula, Cuba.

HEMINGWAY ON STAGE: BRIAN GORDON SINCLAIR

THE HEMINGWAY MONOLOGUES

ORIGINS

The following interview was conducted several years ago by Allie Baker as part of The Hemingway Project. It is reprinted here in its original form:

1. A big part of your career is based on Hemingway. How often do you perform as EH?

   Not as often as I would like. Approximately ten years ago, I started to write one Hemingway play. Now, in 2010, I am starting work on my seventh play. It takes me at least one year to write, memorize and rehearse a single play; consequently, little time is left for extended performances. No one play has been performed more than a dozen times. When the final play is completed for June of 2011, I hope to embark on an extended tour schedule.

2. Originally you didn't know much about Hemingway when you thought about portraying him on stage. What tipped the scale for you in deciding that you would portray him and not someone else?

In 2000, I wrote, directed and performed *Easter Rising: The Last Words of Patrick Pearse*. The play was a dramatic day by day enactment of the Dublin uprising of 1916 as told by the leader of the rebel forces. I had never attempted such an undertaking and was overwhelmed by the positive response. In as much modesty as I can summon, I never thought that I could be that good. I wanted to recreate the experience and I wanted the thrill of portraying another hero on stage. One day, I picked up a copy of *A Farewell to Arms*. Because of my Irish play, I was attracted to the war theme and to the lessons that were displayed in the story but perhaps it was the futility of war that struck me most. "There is no such thing as a good war; there is only war and it only destroys." I was reading an author who had not only experienced war but also understood it with a sensitivity that was deeply and profoundly moving. His adaptation of the Napoleonic retreat and the incorporation of the caesarian birth of son Patrick into the tragic ending convinced me that I was dealing with a great artist.

3. To write and perform a one-actor play, you must feel as if you know Hemingway inside and out. Your plays are in the first person. How did you decide on his voice and tone? Did you listen to tapes of his voice? How did you adapt your own voice to become Hemingway?

Yes, I listened to the available recordings of Hemingway. I listened to the Nobel Prize speech and to the imperfect excerpts compiled by A. E. Hotchner. I also listened to the soundtrack of the film, *The Spanish Earth*. The latter recording is thanks to the fact that Ernest replaced the original narrator, Orson Welles.

No, I did not adapt my voice to imitate Hemingway. I decided to use my own voice. Valerie Hemingway, after seeing one of my plays, said that I captured the spirit and essence of the man. Since she is one of the few remaining people who actually knew Ernest, I consider her comment high praise. The only aspect of my voice that I changed was to place the sound in the middle of my hard palate to create a relatively neutral American sound. Having been trained in classical theatre, I did not want any vestiges of a Shakespearian actor issuing forth from Ernest's mouth, nor did I want any remnants of a distinctly Canadian sound..eh!

The rest of the voice and tone came from a solid belief in performance. I play Ernest as strong and heroic with moments of sublime tenderness. It is this feeling that created the voice and the movement. My job is, as one of my theatre mentors, Jerzy Growtoski, taught me, to blend the character with my own personality, inhabit the character fully and to recreate each performance at will.

4. Tell me about the research you did to write your plays. The details you include of his life are impressive, where did you get it? Biographies, letters, conversations?

    My research was and is no different than the others who have responded to your questions and I would like to add that those responses are quite illuminating. Your project is wonderful and I hope it ends up being published in book form. The different perspectives are wonderful.

I have read every Hemingway text, every biography, every available letter and every anecdote that is readily obtainable. Sadly after, several years, I have also forgotten much of the material. It seems that my head can only hold what is relevant to my current play.

5. What were your favourite sources of material for Hem?

My favourite sources are the actual works and the *Selected Letters*, edited by Carlos Baker. Of the biographical material, I subscribe primarily to Michael Reynolds' superb five-part treatment and I quite like the insights of Scott Donaldson as he breaks the material into topic areas in his book, *By Force of Will: The Life and Art of Ernest Hemingway*.

Another favourite source is the memoirs by those who knew Hemingway. Aside from the usual litany of books, I would like to suggest, *The Best Friend I Ever Had: Revelations about Ernest Hemingway from those who knew him* by David Nuffer and *My Cuban Son: Reflections on the Writer by His Longtime Majordomo* by Rene Villarreal and Raul Villarreal. Although some of the memoirs are not literary masterpieces, these two are obviously written with care, with concern and with great affection. The former interviews people who knew him in both Cuba and Idaho. The latter provides much information about life at Finca Vigia from an insider's point of view. In both cases, we see a gentler, kinder Hemingway than some are used to. I will definitely use certain insights from these two books in my final play.

Conversations with various friends have helped to focus my ideas and have occasionally contributed ideas for my plays; unfortunately, these conversations were considered private and confidential and cannot be discussed here. One of those conversations, however, provided the information on the "missing manuscripts' which I will mention later. I can tell you that in a recent conversation with the Director of Museo Hemingway, I discovered some new information about one of Hemingway's beloved dogs that I was not certain of before. This new information will be incorporated into my new play and may result in a revision to a previous play. I will not tell you what that information is. You will have to discover it in performance. Should you be at the Hemingway Days Festival this July in Key West, I will be pleased to personally answer the question.

One more conversation that was unique occurred in "The Top" rooftop lounge at La Concha Hotel in Key West. The distinguished looking gentleman sitting next to me in the summer of 2003 turned out to be Sir Rex Hunt. He had just arrived with his son who was a pilot and was enjoying a brief vacation. Sir Rex was the Governor of the Falkland Islands when Argentina invaded and Margaret Thatcher sent the British Navy to save him. What I did not know is that Sir Rex was also the Assistant District Commissioner for Uganda in the 50's when Ernest's planes crashed. Sir Rex received a direct report on both crashes including one from Reg Cartwright, the pilot of the second plane and he was instrumental in coordinating the rescue operation. In my possession, hand written by Sir Rex Hunt, is a six page description of what was in the report including specific details of the attempts by Ernest and Mary to exit the plane. Some of these details, I have never heard before. They will also be used in my final play.

6. Your plays seems to capture a sense of humour – is that yours or Hemingway's?

Both...I am a mischievous fellow and it is obvious that in reading the letters of Ernest Hemingway, he suffers from the same magnificent character affliction. Take a look at the letter he writes to his parents about his first trip to Italy. You will get seasick just reading it. Also, have a look at his letter to Scott Fitzgerald about the idea of heaven. It's sexist but it's very funny too.

The sense of humour is also part of the dramatic structure that I create. Didn't we all learn that lesson from old Will Shakers? Always provide comic relief, even in a tragedy. I have worked very hard to incorporate that technique and it seems to work well. It makes Ernest more human and more enjoyable...to play and to watch.

7. What period of Hemingway's life do you find the most interesting?

This question is the most difficult of all. Now that I have lived through most of his life in my plays, I confess to love it all. I must, of course, suggest a slight hesitancy towards those ECT treatments. If forced to narrow in, I would choose the Paris years because they are reminiscent of my own sense of discovery of a world full of wonders. As I discovered the newness of Hemingway, he too discovered the newness of Paris. He was a young romantic learning about life and the craft of writing in one of the most beautiful cities in the world. When I finally got there, I found the vastness of La Gare du Nord and experienced the kindness of strangers. I strolled the streets of Montparnasse and the Left Bank and smelled the irresistible aroma of fine foods that drove Ernest and his hunger into the museum of the Luxembourg Gardens to discover a new sustenance in the paintings of Cezanne and Monet. I shared conversation with a beautiful woman at close tables in Les Deux-Magots and felt the caress of wine and desire. I enjoyed the moment of invitation at a new yet similar Shakespeare and Co. when asked to read from my own work. I sat in the Closerie des Lilas scribbling notes of dreamed brilliance just as Ernest had done years before and the air in my lungs felt clean and good. Whether standing on top of the Eiffel Tower or staring into the shining, rippled darkness of the Seine at night, I felt and I understood that "if you are lucky enough to have lived in Paris as a young man then wherever you go for the rest of your life, it stays with you." Sighhhhhhhhh!

8. For you, what is the most interesting moment in Hemingway's life?

Any moment where Ernest was involved in saving a life is the most interesting of his life.

Currently, I am working on a personal favourite which will be used in my new Hemingway play; consequently, I will not go into detail. In brief, Mary almost died because of the hemorrhaging from a tubular pregnancy. Because of a technique that Ernest learned during the war, he was able to save her. This information is readily available in the biographical works; otherwise, you will have to wait for the stage version to see how I interpret the story.

Another moment that is already present in one of my plays is the time Ernest saved his son Gig from three, huge sharks. It is a rousing, adventure story and illustrates perfectly the compassion that was a large part of Ernest Hemingway. He would have given up his life for his son.

9. I am very eager to hear your theory of the disappearance of Hemingway's manuscripts when Hadley travelled from Paris to Lausanne. Please share it with us.

   This theory has no sound scientific basis and is, in fact, not my theory but the result of a psychic's reading. It is neither dramatic nor has it been used in my play; however, it is a plausible theory and quite reasonable in the circumstances of the time.

   ...Ernest was assigned to cover the Peace Conference in Lausanne, Switzerland and he wanted Hadley to go with him but she caught cold, really bad. They agreed that she would join him later. As soon as she was healthy, she packed her bags. In a separate valise, she packed all of the manuscripts. She figured that Ernest would want to do some writing during the holidays and decided to surprise him. At the Gare de Lyon, she gave her luggage, including the valise to a porter while she bought some Evian water for her throat. When she reached her compartment, her personal bags were there but the valise was missing. Someone had stolen it. All the manuscripts were gone. How did this theft happen? Did the porter take the valise?

According to the psychic, the answer is no. After the First World War, many widows of the soldiers were left with little or no pension. As a gesture, the government provided them with minimal wage jobs as cleaning women in various locations including the train stations. They supplemented their meager income by keeping any lost items they found, an unspoken benefit. The porter, because he had been warned by Hadley, hid the valise under the seat in her compartment, ostensibly for safe keeping but just before Hadley arrived with her water, an old cleaning lady checked the compartment. The bags on the seats were too large and heavy to take readily but when she looked under the seat she saw the smaller valise and made a quick assumption that it had been forgotten there. In her mind, the valise was fair game. She took it, concealed it under her shawl and apron and left. Later, she returned to her dreary, single room shelter and dreamed of the valuables, jewels perhaps, that might be inside the suitcase. Methodically, she lit a small fire in the old pot bellied stove, her only source of heat, with the few twigs and sticks collected from the streets.

Slowly, she opened the bag. Paper, nothing but paper! She lifted the pages, searched in every corner and uttered a sigh of disappointment. No hope remained, only useless pieces of paper. Well, she could get some use out of the contents. Slowly, she crumpled a page and threw it into the fire...then another page and another. One by one the pages of Ernest Hemingway's manuscripts and drafts disappeared into the flames where they turned to black ash. The work of months, years, for a few, brief minutes, provided the little warmth that an old widow would feel on that cold and lonely day.

Many mystery writers have used the missing manuscripts as the basis for a novel. I have read four or five of them. Not a single one is worth the read. Let us instead celebrate the magic and mystery of not knowing.

10. Tell me about the travel you've done on behalf of Ernest Hemingway.

Key West was my first stop. I thought the festival would give me a variety of experiences and it did. After meeting with Robert Charles (Bob) Orlin, I was persuaded to enter the first ever Young Hemingway Contest to be held at Rick's across the street from Sloppy Joe's. The Sloppy Joe's contest was out of the question. I did not have a white beard. With a "younger" look, I won the contest at Rick's and commenced a lifelong friendship with Bob. I fell in love with Key West and formed an ongoing relationship with the Key West Art and Historical Society and their wonderful Executive Director, Claudia Pennington. I am proud to say that I now donate all my festival box-office to the Society. I also have many friends in the Look-alike Society and help raise money for their scholarship fund as well. With friends at Sloppy Joe's, museums, restaurants, stores, media outlets and various other places, I now acknowledge Key West as my second home. Oh yes, I was also presented with $500.00 in cash from Rick's. Turns out this was exactly enough to buy me a plane ticket to Cuba from Canada.

I have now been to Cuba four times and expect to return at least twice in the next year as I prepare to debut a new play. From performances during an eclipse along the Malecon to wild drives through Matanzas and exciting rehearsals with dancers and musicians, I could write a book about the Cuban experience alone. This story is not over.

I have also travelled to Oak Park and Chicago. Seeing the Man-eating Lions of Tsavo and the Rift Valley recreation in the Museum of Natural History helped explain how a desire for adventure in Africa could be aroused in a young boy. Unfortunately, Africa is the main place that I have not visited. I rely, for the time being, on Bob Orlin's exciting accounts of his visits.

In Michigan, I visited the youthful vacation site of Walloon Lake and explored the area around Horton's Bay where Ernest and Hadley were married. At the lake, I waded out and plucked a small stone which, to this day, I carry for luck just as Ernest always carried a lucky piece. I also discovered a church where, it is rumoured, Ernest's young Indian girl friend, Prudy Boulton, is buried in the woods out back. I used this moment to create a scene for one of my plays but I will not tell you about it now. If you see the play, however, I promise that the earth will move for you. Afterwards, I continued up to the Petosky area where the staff at the Little Travers Bay Museum still talks fondly of their "little Ernie" who used to sit and listen intently to the stories told in this former train station. Now, I try to listen a lot too.

Piggott, Arkansas was a pleasant surprise. Everyone wanted to build Ernest a writing studio and the family of Pauline Pfeiffer was no exception. I actually got to stand in a galvanized wash tub where Ernest used to take his sponge baths. The family home is restored, the studio is again restored after a fire and there is a fine gift shop and a nearby education centre. Well worth a visit.

Ketchum, Idaho gave me the opportunity to stand at the Hemingway gravesite and to see how beautiful the area is. Anyone who says Ernest suffered when he came here is not referring to the countryside. A guide at the local museum kindly presented me with a picture of Hemingway kicking a can (his "action" photo), the librarian gave me my first introduction to the FBI files and I sat beside the statue of Ernest that, peacefully tucked beside a flowing stream, reminded me that "...now he is a part of it forever." Later this old Irishman attended a writer's conference at Sun Valley and met Frank McCourt for our first and last conversation. God bless you Frank and God bless Ireland.

Brian Gordon Sinclair

London, England, provided a small, time capsule of Ernest's flights with the Royal Air Force. I managed to visit an airfield museum in Sussex where I saw a Lancaster bomber restored and in flight. Although Ernest went up in Mitchell B-25's, this was close enough to feel what must have been a similar sense of exhilaration. The experience did provide information for my fifth Hemingway play, *The Death Factory*.

Venice, Italy...beautiful beyond belief! I went to the same morning market as Ernest, wrote notes at a desk in the Gritti Palace and ate and drank at Harry's Bar. Harry Cipriani Jr. introduced himself and then stood me up for a scheduled meeting the next day. Even so, I purchased a book that Harry had written about what he, as a child, remembered of Ernest's visits to their home on the small, nearby island of Torcello. Harry claimed that Ernest, in the evening, would get a sixteen bottle case of wine sent to his room. He would then write all night and in the morning sixteen empty bottles would appear outside the door. Amazing what the mind of a child remembers. It's no wonder so many exaggerations have come to be accepted as truth. Thanks a lot Harry! By the way, Harry is now fighting tax evasion charges.

Spain was special and still is. I will be returning in July for a little Hemingway publicity in and near Pamplona. (News Flash! As I am checking this document, two complimentary air tickets from Toronto to Pamplona via Madrid have just arrived in my mailbox courtesy of the Government of Navarre.)

The Hemingway Monologues

If you go out and look at Pamplona
Really look
You must sit in a restaurant that is high
Roof top high
Just before the sun has set.
The sunlight streams and shimmers and slides
Over tiles
Over tiles
And it is pure
And it is beautiful
And it is Pamplona.

No sky is more blue
No man is more warmed
warmed
In Pamplona
In Navarre

(2009: When I completed these simple words at the top of the Hotel Maisonnave, my eyes were wet. I was in Pamplona and I saw what Ernest saw and for a moment I felt like Ernest...and no one should be that lucky.)

My first visit a few years ago was the most exciting. I discovered the bullfight which I will not discuss here. Again, see my play *Death in the Afternoon* in which, like Ernest's book of the same title, I deal with the issue. What I will discuss is the Spanish Civil War. I had the great pleasure of being escorted through the battlefields by the late Tom Entwistle. Tom showed me the untended fields, ignored by General Franco and even considered for sale to Disney as a site for a theme park. A theme park!

Thank God that never happened! In the sides of the hills were dugout quarters where members of the International Brigades had slept. Lying on the ground were pieces of shrapnel, shell casings, rusting food cans and molding pieces of leather boot strap. It was one of those places where, if you closed your eyes and breathed the air, you could smell and sense the spirits of the soldiers still there, still fighting for freedom. I was so moved that I wrote the entire second act of *The Man-Eaters* on this topic. Whenever I perform that play, some of those fragments and casings are with me. "The first American dead have been a part of the earth of Spain for a long time now."

Much more to explore! Much more to write!

11. There is a picture on your website of you and Gregorio Fuentes in Cuba. What was it like to meet him and what did you talk about?

Sadly, Gregorio was near the end of his life when we met. Within a year he would be dead. By this time, he was too frail to hold court at La Terraza Restaurant and collect his free lunches from the tourists. When I arrived at the restaurant and expressed an interest, they relayed the message to Gregorio's grandson with whom he lived a few short blocks from the restaurant. The grandson collected me and took me home where Gregorio came out, sat in a wheelchair and smoked a cigar. This meeting was little more than a photo opportunity as the grandson worked hard to perpetuate the myth that Gregorio was the actual role model for *The Old Man and the Sea*. Gregorio was reduced to monosyllabic comments and dropping burning ash on his trousers. He was 103 years old but no excuses were required for his declining powers. The old captain had lived a long life and his head was still held high with a fine smile on that aged face. He would remain that way until the age of 104. Well lived, Gregorio.

12. Do younger audiences watch your plays? (I noticed some racy parts in the excerpts!) If they do, are they aware of who Ernest Hemingway is?

Generally, I request that my audiences be adult; however, I think that age 16 is a good dividing line. If I am made aware of younger audiences members, I tone down some elements. Ironically, some audiences most critical of the elements of life are adults who have never read the great Nobel Prize winner. Hemingway loved the raunchy parts of life and to present him as otherwise would be to leave out an integral part of his personality. My plays are only mildly racy and those brief moments are mixed with much sensitive and profound thought. Frankly, only a true prude could object.

Today, few young people know much about Hemingway. A recent US poll of secondary school students found that less than 14% could even identify the famous author. On the positive side, I remember two young waitresses who worked at the Casa Marina in Key West. I was fortunate to be sponsored by the hotel and offered the young ladies complimentary tickets to my play. The next day at breakfast, I was greeted by hugs and exclamations.

They had "loved" the show and the first thing they wanted to know was what should they read and where could they buy it. I later caught one reading *A Moveable Feast*. They thought this Hemingway fellow was okay. Well, that's what it's all about, isn't it? Get them interested and get them reading. One day, they may even get to writing.

13. What do you think accounts for the continued interest in Hemingway?

    The actual literature is the key to everything else. If the work were not good, it would not endure. It is readable; it is often profoundly readable and it endures.

    "The secret is that it is poetry turned into prose and that is the hardest of all things to do. It's good enough for you to do it once for a few men to remember you but if you do it year after year then many people will remember and if it's good enough, it will last as long as there are human beings."

    The span of this literature is immense and universal. Ernest writes of a childhood where he sees babies born in violence, teenage years where he looks for sex on piney boughs, love and creation with wives and writing, exciting travel and the slow, inexorable movement towards our end. For every age, for every interest, there is a Hemingway.

    Combine good literature and universality with romantic adventure and you have the elements of the first "rock star" of literature. Ernest is blown up serving chocolate to the troops and saves a life. He camps and hunts and fishes in the Michigan woods. He discovers bullfighting at the Festival of San Fermin. He chases Nazi U-boats and searches for spies in the Caribbean. He sends both himself and ambulances to the anti-fascist cause in Spain. He marches into the death factory that is the Hurtgen Forest in WW II and he captures the great marlins of the Gulf Stream. This is not a life. This is the basis for a thousand stories. Ernest Hemingway lived the equivalent of several lives in his short span and he never ran out of material. What he ran out of was time.

14. You mention being attacked by Romanian gypsies in Pamplona. I just have to ask you about that!

The actual story happened in Madrid. It was my first visit and my guide and friend, Stephen Drake-Jones (Chairman of the Wellington Society), had taken me to a well known street market called El Rastro. When some gypsies started brushing against us, Stephan quickly turned harsh, used the "F" word and shouted and gestured them away. He explained that the area was full of pickpockets and that the Romanian gypsies were the worst offenders. Later, one evening, on my own, I decided to explore a major shopping street near Plaza Mayor. It was filled with tapas bars, ice cream shops, vendors of all sorts and...you got it...more gypsies. In a moment of the utmost stupidity, I turned down a dark side street looking for an apparent shortcut. Instead I found a gypsy encampment. An old oil barrel blazed hellish warmth as a very, rough crowd lay scattered on flattened cardboard boxes and suddenly I was standing in the middle of it. With an agility born of nervousness and fear, I stepped on in that fast gait that tries to look slow and in control. I fooled no one. Every eye was on me but no one moved. Soon, I was around the corner and back in the crowded street of shoppers. I breathed slowly, looked around and saw no one. Being brave was not on my mind. I walked quickly in the direction of the subway. That's when I felt the "butterfly". Something was fluttering around the cuff of my trouser. As I looked down, a face at ground level was withdrawing. His hands had been floating up and down my trousers in an attempt to distract me. At the same time, I felt a tug at the leather shoulder bag I was carrying on the opposite side. With the strength of at least seven Hercules (No, make that eight.), I tightened the grip on the bag and remembered what Stephen Drake-Jones had told me. I drew myself to my full height, still gripping the bag, waved my free arm threateningly and screamed HELP as loudly as I could. I then shouted, POLICIA, POLICIA, pointed a finger at the two culprits and continued shouting, THIEF, PUTA (whore), F__K OFF! By this time, every shopper, every shop owner was staring. The thieves slinked back and with extended palms, made a gesture of conciliation. For a moment, all was still and then I gestured them away. Thankfully, they disappeared into the darkness. One more second of quiet and the crowd erupted into applause. Suddenly, briefly, I was a hero...and I have never felt more like Ernest Hemingway than at that precise moment. Of course, I quickly smartened up and got the hell out.

107

Later when I related the incident to Stephen, he complimented me in the usual expert manner, "That was really a dumb thing to do, Brian." I agreed and promised not to walk alone in dangerous areas, even if I did know the secret words. For whatever reason, whore and the "F" word are particularly offensive to the gypsies.

I did meet some other gypsies in Pamplona but they were simple con artists. They travel in pairs, two women. One precedes the other with a sprig of juniper which she gives to you in an apparent gesture of good will. The second woman then approaches with a story of luck attached to the juniper and proceeds to tell your fortune. When finished, she makes it obvious that you are expected to pay. If you refuse, the second woman joins in and the harassment is loud and embarrassing. Most people pay to get rid of them. When I was approached my guide and translator was with me so the foregoing situation did not materialize. We did, however chat about luck and I showed them my lucky Hemingway stone from Walloon Lake. Immediately, one of the women shouted, "Oh, good luck!" and snatched the stone from my hand. She then lifted her dress in each of those very private areas and rubbed the stone thoroughly over breasts and groin. When finished, the other woman repeated the process and returned the stone with many thanks for sharing my luck. When I returned to Canada and told the story to my wife, she said strongly and clearly, "Wash that stone and wash it now".

15. On a travel forum for Spain, one man wrote "Hemingway has fallen out of favour in Spain. He

was associated with another time as has bullfighting." Do you agree with this?

I can only note that many parts of Spain currently oppose the continuation of bullfighting, at least in its current form. Recent polls show that only 30% of Spanish people approve of bullfighting. In Catalonia, over 180,000 signatures filled a petition to outlaw the practice. The government, however, subsidizes bullfighting, the royal family is divided on the subject and many supporters remain from the Franco regime which promoted bullfighting as essentially and uniquely Spanish.

My experience has not been with the opponents of the bullfight. In Madrid, I attended and studied the art of the corrida. My attitude prior to this visit was negative. Afterwards, I became a convert. Not only was I enthralled by the pageantry but I was impressed by the quick dispatch of the meat, some to restaurants and much to the needy. The death of the bull, after a lifetime of luxury, was more humane than many of the slaughters that put food on our tables. And, of course, the bull got to fight back. Just ask Jose Tomas whose recent goring made international headlines. I was also amazed at the surgical precision of the on-site abattoir. Clinically dressed and armed with samurai-like tools, the staff skinned and prepared the meat for delivery in a matter of minutes. It was clean, it was efficient and it is what you do to meat in order to eat. Hmm...didn't really mean to get into this issue but I am a convert. Many will never be converts. I know this and Ernest knew this.

If Pamplona is any example, Ernest Hemingway is as popular as ever. They recently held an international look-alike contest. 7000 people crowded the Plaza del Castillo to watch. When I was there for the Running of the Bulls, people would pass in the streets and shout, "Hello, Hemingway." In a restored palace, a large display of poster size photos from Hemingway's last visit drew healthy crowds. I was also presented with a published book containing Hemingway's *Toronto Daily Star* article on Pamplona in both English and Spanish. Believe me, Hemingway is alive and well in Pamplona.

16. How have you incorporated or dealt with Hemingway's tendency to exaggerate and tell lies?

The great English actor, Lord Laurence Olivier, once stated that an actor's career is based on his ability to lie. Like Olivier, Hemingway often changed a truth into a dramatic lie for the sake of his writing. In his public life he was prone to some lies and much exaggeration.

As a young man, he spoke to a high school audience and suggested that he served with the blood thirsty Arditi in Italy. These soldiers were so tough that, when wounded, they would stuff the wounds with cigarette butts and keep on fighting. As a former liar and as an embellisher of dramatic moments, I have seen the truth of lies in my own character. Look inside your own youthful memories. How many times did you lie or exaggerate in the service of your developing ego. For famous authors, those exaggerations become further exaggerated through a constant retelling and reshaping by secondary sources.

In my play, *The Death Factory*, I deal with some of Ernest's WW II extenuations of the truth. How's that for a euphemism? I tell of commanding a group of partisans called his "irregular cavalry," of storing arms in his room at Rambouillet, of issuing orders through a US army colonel, of liberating the Ritz Hotel and Shakespeare and Company and I show him defending himself to the Inspector General. Yes, he lied to the Inspector General but the lies were based on positive actions. Hemingway was an excellent scout, a tough interrogator and a man capable of true leadership. His work did help prepare the way for the Free French Forces. I have fun with these exaggerations but, always, I return to a man with many heroic attributes.

I also intend to look at the lie of self-deception in my final play. Ernest easily succumbed to the folly of flattery and a pretty face as witnessed through both romance and marriage. It is at an older age, however, that he builds a sad, personal fantasy. He did not age well and, like so many of us, he wanted to capture a youth that was lost; consequently, he formed an unrealistic attachment to the young Italian countess, Adriana Ivancich. My studies have uncovered some eyewitness accounts of Adriana that will clearly reveal her side of the relationship. I will present those views in the play.

I do not approve of lying. I did too much of it as a young man and I finally learned the hard lesson of the damage that is done. In my plays and in the stories of Ernest Hemingway, however, I absolutely revel in the grandness of the exaggeration and I attempt to present it as a glorious and joyous attempt to make life bigger and richer than it might otherwise be.

17. What is the best part about playing Hemingway over and over again?

It is wonderful to have a best friend. Like a child with an imaginary playmate, a playwright lives inside his head. As an actor, I expand this inner reality into words and performance. Often, I feel as if I am sharing the stage with all the people in Ernest's life and with Ernest himself.

When I get it right, the performance that is, I feel an extremely strong bond with my audience. We are, in that unique Zen way, at one and for them I become Ernest.

18. One of the benefits of having an interest in Hemingway seems to be the forming of friendships with Hemingway aficionados all over the world. Has this been true for you? Tell me about the friendships you've made because of EH.

I have made and continue to keep many friends through my Hemingway endeavours. Here are two friends and I apologize to the many I have not mentioned:

Lorian Hemingway – Lorian is an exceptional talent and I am both proud and humbled to say that we have helped each other on numerous occasions. Her

Short Story Competition is one of the best in the world and each year I enjoy either hearing or reading the winning entry. Lorian is a very special friend and it is our spoken and unspoken understanding of her grandfather that makes this friendship special..

Bob and Debbie Orlin – Aside from their own fine talents, Bob and Debbie joined me in the presentation of my very first Hemingway play in Key West. They prompted, helped with set-up, worked security and provided complete moral support. Bob and Debbie have never let me down and they have worked every show that I have presented in Key West. Hemingway said that the best way to find out if you can trust people is to trust them. I have found someone to trust.

I have also had the pleasure of being assisted by many Canadian Embassies and Consulates throughout the world. Because of policy and confidentially, I will not mention any names here. Know though that some of these people have become close, personal friends. I have also formed a strong and positive bond with the Consul General of Cuba.

19. You have seven separate Hemingway plays – which one is your favourite to perform? Why?

Honestly, I have no favourite. Because of the chronological approach, I view the plays as one long continuum. Briefly, I will mention a point of personal enjoyment for each play:

The Hemingway Monologues

Hemingway On Stage

Part I – Sunrise: The Early Years

At the end of this play, I talk about the death of Catherine Barkley and her child in *A Farewell to Arms*. When the lights come up for the curtain call, there is not a dry eye in the house. For an actor, this is a humbling moment of dramatic power.

Part II – The Lost Generation

When I speak of Ezra Pound, I digress and explain how Ernest worked to have him freed from a mental hospital and even provided some money for Ezra to return to Italy. It is the compassion of such deeds that impress me.

(In Venice, I discovered that Ezra is buried on Cemetery Island.)

Part III – Death in the Afternoon

I actually hired a bullfighting aficionado to coach me for an onstage recreation of the bullfight. This gentleman had trained for the corrida but he told me that he lacked the true courage needed to face the bulls. I too could never face a bull but as an actor, I can. What a thrill to wield the banderillas, to spin the capa or capote in a veronica, to carefully hold the muleta before the estoque or sword is inserted...and then to finally....guess you'll have to see the ending.

Part IV – The Man-Eaters

My plays are subtitled, *The Road to Freedom*. Here, I devote an act to the Spanish Civil War and there is a heartfelt pleasure in portraying a struggle devoted to stopping Hitler and Mussolini.

Part V – The Death Factory

Although the same fight for freedom continues from the previous play, I deal with Ernest's relationship with his son Jack or Bumby in this play. I enjoy playing the compassionate father who truly cares for his children.

(Part VI – Sunset: In Deadly Ernest

This play was not completed at the time of the interview.)

Part VII - Special Edition – Hemingway's HOT Havana
This special edition play is not a part of the chronological series. It was created to blend with some Cuban music and dance but works well as a stand alone presentation of stories. I always have a great deal of fun when I do this show. The audience must enjoy it too. Key West has asked for a return engagement at this year's Hemingway Days Festival in July.

20. You tell me about some of the Hemingway Festivals and events you've attended. Certainly they must differ from Key West to Norway – do they celebrate different aspects of EH?

I have to point out that I have never been to a Hemingway Festival other than Key West. I have been to certain literary festivals where Ernest was honoured. For Instance:

The Stratford-upon-Avon International Festival of Literature - A featured theme of this festival was a celebration of the "angry young man" of British writing. Fortunately for me, the director of the festival, Steve Newman, was a Hemingway fan and felt the name would draw some added attention. Colin Wilson, author of *The Outsider* and one of the original "angry young men," paid me the great compliment of asking for an autographed copy of my script. He was more interested in Hemingway than anything else. I wasn't even angry.

Ordkalotten International Festival of Literature, Tromso, Norway – The director of this festival, Lene E. Westeras had seen one of my performances in her travels and invited me to participate in the theme of the festival – violence in literature. I had the pleasure of helping open the festival with excerpts from *The Death Factory* and later, I gave a full performance of the Havana play. On the last day of the festival, I conducted a session on the machismo of Hemingway. Interestingly, many were interested in the sad ending of son Gregory's life and what level of latent homosexuality could be applied to Ernest. Being Scandinavian they were very open to all concepts. Another conversation involved a lady who was had visited Finca Vigia in Cuba. I was later told that she was the leading candidate for Minister of Culture in the next election. Indeed, Ernest has fans everywhere.

21. In one write up, you say, "Spiritually, I have become a friend of Ernest Hemingway and Ernest and I will be friends forever." I think you have hit on something that a lot of people feel when they become truly immersed in his life. In fact, many of the people I talk to spend an enormous amount of time and money on this relationship they make with Ernest Hemingway. My blog and your plays, Bob Orlin's paintings and the Hemingway sites and discussion boards – these are all labours of love. Can you expound on why this is so?

This question is reminiscent of others where you asked about the continued interest in Hemingway. The life of Ernest Hemingway detailed the events of the first half of a century. He was born into "interesting times" in a town of "broad lawns and narrow minds." As he escaped his limitations and lived through the years he became a symbol for everything that is missing in most of our lives of "quiet desperation". Today, I travel the world primarily because of Ernest. Both research and performance provide opportunities that were very limited in the past and are now constantly expanding. Ernest Hemingway gives me a richness of soul that I never fully possessed before. His life, in a sense, is like a guidebook on how to be a man. Some chapters are from the Boy Scouts, some are from the manual of war and others offer much understanding and exploration of relationships. If you read this life carefully, very carefully, you will note that many mistakes were made but if you are wise enough, you will see much evidence of the development of the compassionate nature. I cannot speak for others but I can say, without equivocation, I am a better person because of my relationship with Ernest Hemingway.

22. In another interview for the *Miami Herald*, you say, "Hemingway has become my hero. You cannot write with his sensitivity and be the person he's accused of being: a womanizing, alcohol-abusing man with bad behaviour. He's very complex creating more than most of us will in 10 lifetimes." How do you reconcile some of those things that Hemingway is accused of?

For every human being, there is a time to be weak and a time to be strong. What defines us is the strength of our caring. Whenever I read too many articles, especially those cheap Hemingway mystery novels that immerse themselves in negativity, I think of two things, two letters written by Ernest:

The first letter was sent to Gerald and Sara Murphy after the death of their young son, Baoth, at age 15 from meningitis. Ernest wrote that letter with a deep compassion that provides immense insight into the act of grieving and into the loss of anyone whom you have loved. Most of all, I was moved by his advice for continuing and living life, "We must live it, now, a day at a time and we must be very careful not to hurt each other."

The second letter came near the end of Ernest's life and was sent from the Mayo Clinic. It was to Fritz (Frederick) Saviers, the nine year old son of Dr. George Saviers. Fritz was in a Denver hospital and suffering from viral heart disease. The boy would live another six years. Ernest would be dead in two and a half weeks but he spoke of meeting and joking about their hospital experiences together.

It is very important to know that you can make a decision about your own life...a deadly decision, in deadly "Ernest"...but it doesn't have to make you feel any different about the lives of others. You can still care and hope and Ernest always knew that a child's life was precious.

These letters give me my solace. These letters give me my belief in the goodness of Ernest Hemingway.

23. Do you think your plays help dispel some of the myths about Ernest Hemingway? Your plays seem to have tapped into the more gentle or noble parts of Hemingway's personality. Was this deliberate on your part, were you trying to dispel some of the stereotype of him and was this truly the man you found as you did your research.

Much of this question has been dealt with in my previous responses but the main myth I dispel is the misconception that Hemingway would write while drunk. I love to point out the discipline of someone who, for much of his life, would rise at dawn and write until lunch. It is that discipline that allowed the production of great literature. What I will add is that I truly wanted to find a noble Hemingway. Anyone, in examining a life so vast, can find anything that satisfies a particular end or interpretation. My end was nobility and I found it. My Hemingway is a hero!

24. Tell me about the feedback you get from your plays.

I have received two negative criticisms. Once, a group of religious fundamentalists said that my work was vulgar. This reaction was based on two things, the use of phrases like "son of a bitch" and references to the fact that Ernest had sex. I now check I.D. at the door. If their driver's license has the letters RF, the owner is refused entry and given a free ticket to Creation Land. The other criticism came from a group of recovering mental patients. They did not mind the vulgar aspects. They did, however, object to the perceived sexist attitude toward women. Strangely, they laughed, applauded and gave me a standing ovation. Only later, after some conversation amongst themselves did they post a notice saying that my play supported abuse and that it reminded them of the horrors of their own relationships. Since I thought they had viewed a comedy and distinctly remembered their robust laughter, I was surprised to discover that I had written a tragedy. I don't think William Shakespeare ever had this problem.

Otherwise, the feedback is consistently positive. I am meticulous about my work and a perfectionist. Before any show faces an audience it is fully rehearsed and previewed. That's when the flaws are worked out. Each play requires both writing and acting. If you don't rewrite and redirect the acting, the result will be weak. Much of the success is just plain hard work.

The greatest compliment I ever receive is when another professional comes up after a show and says that he or she was transported. That word means that they were totally involved in the play and that the performance was totally believable. Another way of stating this is to say that the audience forgets the play as a play and becomes fully involved in the story and the action. Critical faculties are set aside because of the involvement. Sometimes an average audience member will tell me that for a time, he genuinely believed that I was Ernest Hemingway.

I am also amazed at how many people ask about Ernest's writing after seeing my plays. They constantly tell me of being inspired to go out and read the works of the master.

For more specific comments, I suggest that you visit my website:

www.briangordonsinclair.com

25. You gently corrected me on the ehemingway forum about the word "fanatic". What is an aficionado?

First, we must look at Ernest's definition of "aficionado" in the glossary of *Death in the Afternoon*:

- one who understands bullfights in general and in detail and still cares for them.

In North America, the word has moved into a more general usage but still with a strong element of knowledge.

Webster defines "aficionado" as a person who knows about and appreciates a usually fervently pursued interest or study.

The gentleman who coached me in the art of bullfighting was an "aficionado". He understood all the moves of the matador but would never be able to perform them professionally as a matador. He knew every aspect of the corrida but would forever be an amateur, albeit an exceedingly well informed amateur.

"Fanatic" is defined as a person with an extreme and uncritical enthusiasm or zeal, as in religion or politics; often intense, uncritical devotion.

The key word here is "uncritical" Need I say more?

26. If you could do anything with EH, what would it be – betting on horses, fishing for marlin, patrolling for U-boats?

None of the above. If I could, I would meet with Ernest, and share some of the modern understanding of alcohol, of depression and of the side effects of various medications. Might even suggest avoiding a barbaric technique called ECT. But I cannot do that.

Since I cannot do the above, I might as well ask for something else, much simpler, that can happen, at least it can happen in my imagination. All I would ask is to sit quietly with Ernest on the deck of his boat, the Pilar, calmed by a gentle breeze floating over a peaceful view of a beautiful blue Gulf Stream. We would share cool drinks, sigh a few sighs and I would look at him and say, with the utmost affection, "Well done, old friend, well done."

27. Brian, is there anything else you would like to add?

Let me end with one of your favourite Hemingway quotes:

"As you get older, it is harder to have heroes but it is sort of necessary."

Brian Gordon Sinclair: Hemingway On Stage 2010

Coming soon!

PART IV OF THE HEMINGWAY MONOLOGUES:

THE MAN-EATERS

The New Atlantian Library

NewAtlantianLibrary.com
or AbsolutelyAmazingEbooks.com
or AA-eBooks.com

www.ingramcontent.com/pod-product-compliance
Lightning Source LLC
LaVergne TN
LVHW051840080426
835512LV00018B/2983